D0328781

PEACE IS POSSIBLE

PEACE IS POSSIBLE

Conversations with Arab and Israeli Leaders from 1988 to the Present

S. DANIEL ABRAHAM

Foreword by PRESIDENT BILL CLINTON

Newmarket Press • *New York*

HICKSVILLE PUBLIC LIBRARY
169 JERUSALEM AVENUE
HICKSVILLE, NY 11801

Copyright © 2006 by S. Daniel Abraham

Foreword by Bill Clinton copyright © 2006 by Bill Clinton

All rights reserved. This book may not be reproduced, in whole or in part, in any form, without written permission. Inquiries should be addressed to Permissions Department, Newmarket Press, 18 East 48th Street, New York, NY 10017.

This book is published in the United States of America.

First Edition

ISBN-13: 978-1-55704-702-1
ISBN-10: 1-55704-702-2

10 9 8 7 6 5 4 3 2 1

Library of Congress Cataloging-in-Publication Data

Abraham, S. Daniel.
  Peace is possible : conversations with Arab and Israeli leaders from 1988 to the present / by S. Daniel Abraham ; introduction by Bill Clinton.— 1st ed.
      p. cm.
  Includes index.
  ISBN 1-55704-702-2 (cloth : alk. paper)
  1. Arab-Israeli conflict—1993—-Peace. I. Title.
  DS119.76.A3482 2005
  956.05'3—dc22
                                        2005030163

QUANTITY PURCHASES
Companies, professional groups, clubs, and other organizations may qualify for special terms when ordering quantities of this title. For information, write Special Sales Department, Newmarket Press, 18 East 48th Street, New York, NY 10017; call (212) 832-3575; fax (212) 832-3629; or e-mail info@newmarketpress.com.

www.newmarketpress.com

Manufactured in the United States of America.

956.053
A

For the late Congressman Wayne Owens, one of the most remarkable people I have ever met, and the man responsible for opening the Middle East to me, and showing me the possibility that there could be peace, at a time when I was sure there couldn't. Wayne was also a beloved friend. He is deeply, deeply missed every day.

CONTENTS

Photographs follow page 110.

FOREWORD

PRESIDENT BILL CLINTON

For as long as I've known him, Dan Abraham has believed that Palestinians and Israelis can share the land of their fathers together, and for more than fifteen years he has devoted his life to making that dream a reality. Along with the late Congressman Wayne Owens, he has worked tirelessly to keep lines of communication open between both Israeli and Palestinian leaders.

Those fifteen years haven't been easy, and a lesser man might have given up hope of ever achieving peace. Not Dan Abraham—he never stopped thinking success was attainable, and he never stopped striving to achieve a lasting settlement.

Wayne and Dan made over sixty visits to the Middle East and held more than one thousand meetings with leaders from both sides of the conflict, striving to create the common ground and mutual understanding without which peace is impossible.

In *Peace Is Possible,* Dan recounts his fascinating experiences visiting Israel and the Arab world, his impressions of virtually all the heads of state and other government officials he met in his travels, and his own recommendations on how to achieve a lasting resolution, with the Palestinian people able to forge their own destiny and Israel safe and secure, with recognized borders and peaceful, normal relations with their neighbors for the first time in its history. Abraham offers a unique perspective gained from personal interactions with the major figures of the region, and he analyzes the conflict with intelligence and insight. When peace finally comes to the Middle East, it will be because of people like Dan.

—October 2005

Maps

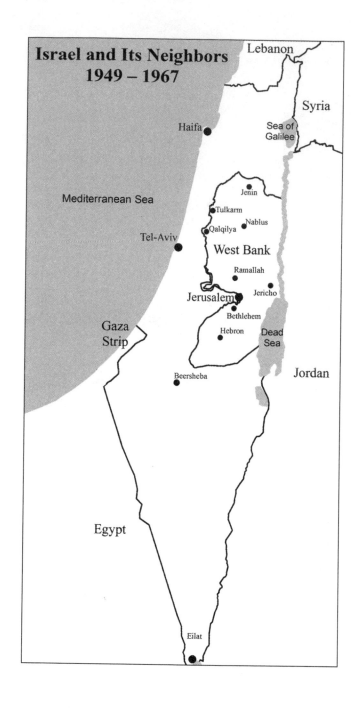

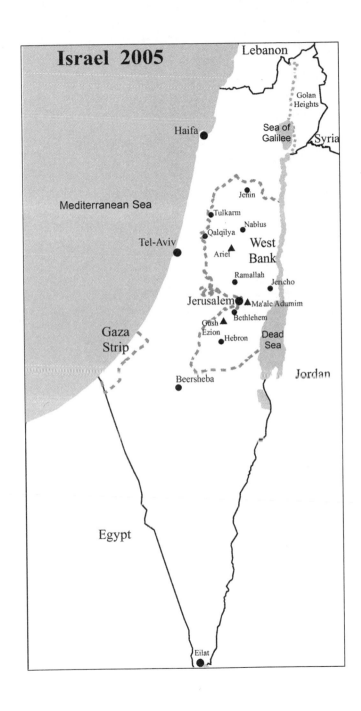

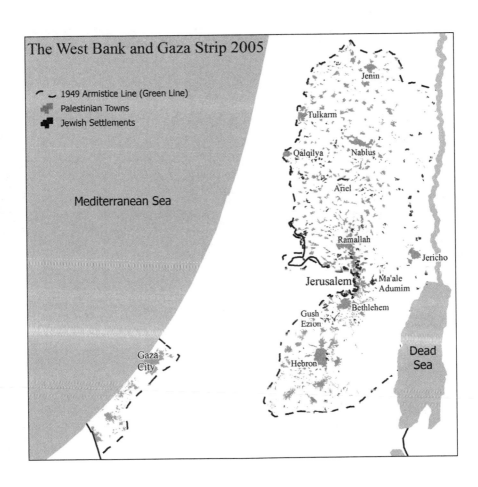

The West Bank and Gaza Strip 2005

- ⌐ ⌐ 1949 Armistice Line (Green Line)
- Palestinian Towns
- Jewish Settlements

Mediterranean Sea

Jenin

Tulkarm

Qalqilya   Nablus

Ariel

Ramallah

Jericho

Jerusalem   Ma'ale Adumim

Bethlehem
Gush
Ezion

Gaza
City

Hebron

Dead
Sea

INTRODUCTION

I am an uncompromising optimist, particularly about a region of the world that usually brings out people's most pessimistic inclinations—Israel and its neighbors. Pessimism belongs to those who have given up.

I belong to neither the camp of the pessimists nor the camp of the vengeful. I'm a committed, passionate Jew, who believes deeply in Rabbi Hillel's age-old one-sentence definition of Judaism's essence: "What is hateful unto you, don't do unto your neighbor. The rest is commentary." We, as Jews, don't want to be occupied by others, and so we should not occupy others. As will be asserted throughout this book, it's not only bad for the people under occupation, it is also bad for the occupier, economically, morally, and in other, surprising ways as well.

And, as regards the camp of the pessimists, I certainly have not given up on the prospects of peace; it is today within our grasp. There are enough significant figures on both sides of the political divide who are eager to make peace happen.

Not in a century, and not in twenty-five years. But now.

I realize that to many my words might sound like those of a visionary. I'm not. I'm a hardheaded business-man who, having made a success in that area of life, turned my attention to the most intractable political problem in the world today, the Israeli/Arab, more specif-ically, the Israeli/Palestinian, conflict. And when I say that peace is attainable now, I am basing it on fifteen years of intimate meetings with the most significant fig-ures in Israel and the Arab world. And these meetings, particularly those in the Arab world, have led me to con-clude that there are people out there, far more than most Israelis and American Jews are willing to acknowledge, who are ready to make peace with Israel.

One hundred years ago, at a time when Zionism seemed remote, and a Jewish state an impossible dream, Theodore Herzl electrified the Jewish people with the words, "If you will it, it is no dream." These words of Herzl apply with equal force today: "If we will peace, it is no dream."

How I have come to these conclusions, and what we can do about them, is the subject of this book.

ONE

The Start of the Journey

My first meeting with Wayne Owens happened at a pro-Israel event, an AIPAC (American Israel Public Affairs Committee) dinner. AIPAC has long been the most effective American political action group on behalf of Israel, and that evening—it was in November 1987—many of AIPAC's elite supporters were paying $300 a plate to come to New York's Pierre Hotel to hear analyses of Israel's political and security situation and to mingle with senators and congressmen.

The congressional representatives were there to reassure Jewish activists of their steadfast commitment to Israel's security, and to garner support for their political campaigns.

I was host of a table, one of whose guests I was informed was a freshman congressman from Utah, a man named Wayne Owens. Many regarded Owens, a devout Mormon, as an important newcomer to the House, as he was a member of the powerful Foreign Affairs Committee.

And me? I was then a sixty-five-year-old bachelor and father of four daughters, who was as interested in catching up with my friends and chatting with the many attractive women in attendance that night than with discussing the intricacies of foreign policy legislation pending before Congress. But at some point pretty late in the evening, I started to talk with Owens about something that was uppermost on my mind that night. "Congressman," I said, "the most important problem America is facing today is homelessness in the streets of big cities. How can I—or anybody—go to a warm, comfortable apartment in New York City and step over the bodies of people sleeping on the streets with no place to go? And it is impossible for any private citizen to do anything significant about it. I can give them a couple of bucks, but that can't solve the problem. It is undignified, it is demeaning, for people to have to live like that, and it is not right for a rich nation like America to permit people to be homeless, especially in wintertime."

Wayne, knowing how seriously Jews took events such as the AIPAC dinner, might have been surprised that I suddenly raised this issue. But it was critical to me. Homelessness was what I witnessed daily when I walked to and from work, and the issue was starting to consume me. I wanted to do something to help solve it. Wayne, I soon learned, had just cosponsored the McKinney Act, a bill intended to help curb homelessness. But from our brief encounter, I could sense that, for him, the issue was still somewhat theoretical; I doubted that he had ever encountered a homeless person face to face, and I wanted him to see the problem firsthand. Within minutes, the two of us left the AIPAC event, and were driving through the wet streets of Manhattan.

I asked the driver to take us to one of the areas in Manhattan where homeless people could be found. Soon, we were crawling Manhattan's darkest neighborhoods— at midnight, no less, and at a time when the city was a lot less safe than it is today—waking and interviewing people who were sleeping in the street. I'm sure we made a curious sight, two men in tuxedos emerging out of a limousine and going over to people lying in the streets.

One man we met that night still sticks in my mind. He was dozing on a rapidly disintegrating cardboard box. I knelt down alongside him, and gently shook him awake. "This is Wayne Owens," I told him. "A congressman from Utah. He wants to know how and why you got here, and whether you are hungry."

The man was more than willing to open up. Indeed, he was cold and hungry, but he was afraid to go to a shelter; he didn't relish the thought of being locked in with people who might be dangerous. And just as sadly, he was too embarrassed to go back to his family and own up to them about what a failure he'd become. "I just can't go home," he told us. I stuffed a twenty into his pocket while he continued to explain to Wayne what made him behave as he did.

We had four such encounters that night. And when it was all over, I took Wayne out to a bar for a drink, where I quickly learned that a Diet Coke was the strongest beverage this pious Mormon would put into his mouth. My tastes were a bit stronger but, nonetheless, that night our friendship began. We could sense right away that, different as we were, we cared a lot about some very similar things. Two weeks later, though, when Wayne called to invite me to accompany him and his wife on a trip to the

Middle East, I told him that I would have loved to go with him—Israel mattered greatly to me—but I had made a commitment to my children to go on a ski trip with them at the same time, and I didn't feel right breaking it.

When Wayne returned from that trip, it was immediately apparent that the experience had deeply affected him. In particular, he had been shaken, and frightened, by a meeting with nearly a hundred angry young Palestinians at Aqbat Jaber, a refugee camp outside Jericho; they had surrounded his car and talked to him with great fury about how badly the Israelis were treating them. Wayne, although passionately committed to Israel's security, felt that their complaints and resentment had to be taken seriously.

Back in Washington, he told Lee Hamilton, the House's chairman of the Europe and Middle East Subcommittee on Foreign Affairs, that he wanted to focus his attention on the Middle East, particularly on Israel and her neighbors. He then called and told me that he was planning a second trip to the region and invited me again to come with him: "I want to see the Middle East through your eyes," is how he put it. He wasn't sure what to make of the anti-Israeli rhetoric he had heard throughout his trip, but he certainly wanted to have the perspective of a highly committed pro-Israel supporter to balance it. Wayne outlined the trip he intended to make, to Egypt and Jordan as well as Israel and the West Bank.

This time, I told him that I would accompany him. I was excited at the thought of making such a trip, but I assumed it was the sort of trip I would really enjoy, accomplish some good, and learn a lot. But not more.

That day, Wayne Owens became my traveling partner. Over the next fifteen years, we made over sixty visits to the Middle East—to Israel, the West Bank and Gaza, Saudi Arabia, Egypt, Syria, Lebanon, Jordan, Bahrain, Morocco, Algeria, Tunisia, the United Arab Emirates, Kuwait, Iraq, Qatar, Oman, and Yemen—eventually logging well over a million miles. We held over a thousand meetings—more than a dozen meetings with President Hosni Mubarak of Egypt, almost as many with President Hafez Assad in Syria—and well over fifty lunches, dinners, and postmidnight meetings with Yasser Arafat and his associates, and countless meetings and discussions with Israeli prime ministers Yitzhak Shamir, Yitzhak Rabin, Shimon Peres, Benjamin Netanyahu, Ehud Barak, and Ariel Sharon.

That first trip quickly turned into a quest for peace that also became the greatest adventure of my life. Even before that trip had ended, I realized that many of my basic assumptions about the Arab world and the chances for peace between Israel and her neighbors were wrong. Profoundly wrong. There could be peace between Israel and the Arab world, I now knew. I also knew that few people then agreed with my assessment, which is why I have devoted my life ever since to trying to make this peace happen.

That first night that Wayne and I met and visited homeless people in the streets of New York set the tone for the next fifteen years of our relationship; ultimately, our quest for a Middle East peace was rooted in the desire to secure a safe homeland for the Jewish people, who had been homeless for 2,000 years, and to likewise secure an independent homeland for the Palestinians.

TWO

The Question of Borders:
Meeting with Mubarak

That first trip, in April 1988, started in Athens. Actually, I was supposed to meet Wayne in Cairo, but there was no way I would go to Egypt by myself. My perception of the Arab world's attitude toward Israel and Jews was frightening. And so I arranged to meet Wayne in Greece so that we could fly over to Egypt together.

But the first fright I experienced in Egypt had nothing to do with my being Jewish. The American ambassador to Egypt, Frank Wisner, had arranged for Wayne and me to meet with Egyptian president Hosni Mubarak. Wisner spent the early morning briefing us on the complexities of Middle East politics; it was an impressive and comprehensive introduction, told with the thrills and drama of a top-notch documentary. His essential thesis was simple: The Egyptian leadership—which a decade earlier had made a peace agreement with Israel—was a force for moderation in the Arab world but, nonetheless, much of the populace (what later came to be known as "the Arab street") was steeped in political extremism and rage against Israel and the West.

By 9 A.M., we set off for the presidential palace in a four-car entourage, with security guards manning the front and back vehicles. Wisner and Wayne were in the second car, a luxury Mercedes, while I was seated with Wayne's staff in the third car. Cairo's traffic, as I quickly learned, is notorious for moving erratically or not moving at all, and Ambassador Wisner ordered the sirens activated. Soon we were zigzagging through Cairo traffic at what seemed like ninety mph, and holding on to our seats so as not to be thrown in the air by the bumps in the road. It was definitely one of the wildest rides of my life, and as frightening as anything I had experienced since serving as a soldier in World War II.

I remember our convoy skidding to a halt behind a stalled driver. Within seconds, an assault rifle was poking out the door of our lead vehicle. The security guard didn't even bother speaking to the stalled driver; he just motioned with the rifle's muzzle for the man to move. How he expected a stalled car to move—with or without a gun pointing at it—I couldn't fathom, but within seconds we had forged ahead and the stalled car was far behind us. Ambassador Wisner explained to Wayne, who later passed this on to me, that, for security reasons, we could not slow down; we were simply too tempting a target for radicals.

That fear I could understand. Only a few years earlier, Islamic fundamentalists had gunned down Egyptian president Anwar Sadat as he sat in a viewing stand at a military parade honoring what Egyptians liked to label their 1973 "victory" over Israel. But that of course is not why the fundamentalists murdered Sadat. It was in part for his historic 1977 trip to Jerusalem and ensuing peace treaty with Israel (also, because he stood in the way of an Islamic state). In return for peace, Israeli prime minister Menachem Begin returned every inch of land that Egypt had lost to Israel in the Six-Day War of 1967, land that had more than doubled Israel's size, and contained oil wells that generated billions of dollars. But to the world of Muslim fundamentalists and political extremists, this diplomatic coup of Sadat was irrelevant. Indeed, Sadat's action had thrown Egypt into pariah status in the Arab world. She had been expelled from the Arab League, and her pariah status among Arab states endured until the end of the 80s.

We finally arrived at the president's palace in Theopolis. Wayne and the ambassador were led inside, but I was told I couldn't come in. The reason I was barred had nothing to do with my being Jewish. Mubarak intended to have a candid discussion with two high-level U.S. officials—an ambassador and a congressman—and I did not have clearance. That was sufficient reason to keep me out. But later, when a second effort was made to exclude me from meeting with the president, Wayne, with the loyalty, guts, and perseverance that I came to so value, argued and argued with Mubarak's staff until they relented and let me in. As Wayne told them, we were a team and he wasn't going to let us be separated.*

Although I later developed a warm and constructive relationship with President Mubarak, I didn't speak

---

* What follows is actually a summary of two meetings held with Mubarak, the first on April 6, 1988, the second on December 13, 1989. Obviously, all my personal observations about, and impressions of, Mubarak are drawn from this second meeting, while the content of the first meeting was conveyed to me by Wayne immediately after the meeting's conclusion.

much at the first meeting I had with him, but somehow, even then, I didn't feel the need to hold back anything. I told him that I was a Jew with a strong commitment to the security of Israel, that I owned a home there, and that I had children living there as well. I also emphasized that I was an American, and had fought in the American army in World War II. My most important priority now, though, and the reason I had come on this trip, was to help Israel and the Arabs find a peaceful road together.

Despite my heartfelt mini-speech, Mubarak didn't react much to what I said; I gather he pretty much saw me as a tag-a-long to a congressman. Which made sense. After all, Mubarak's motive for granting the meeting was to maintain good relations with the American Congress and State Department, not to hear the views of an American-Jewish businessman who had lived in Israel.

I, on the other hand, was immediately impressed by Mubarak's presence, particularly his tremendous sense of personal dignity. It emanated from the cut of his crisp, dark suit, the stern long line of his mouth, and even from his hard jaw. Throughout the meeting, he maintained the posture of the fighter pilot he had once been.

Everything I saw that morning was consistent with what I later learned about him. Mubarak's reputation throughout Egypt was as a man of unbending character. Many years earlier, when President Nasser's brother, Hussein, tried to use his blood ties to skip paying tuition to the flight academy, Mubarak had sent him packing. Later, when President Sadat's brother, Atef, requested preferential treatment, Mubarak forced the cadet to fly more hours than his classmates. When Egypt attacked Israel in the 1973 war, Atef was one of the first pilots shot down.

Given that Mubarak had the reputation of being a lot

less enthusiastic than Sadat had been about the peace process with Israel, I was particularly struck by one comment that he made during our meeting. It was sort of a mea culpa over what he regarded as a mistake Egypt had made: forcing the country's Jews to leave in 1948 and again in 1956. The thrust of his remarks—I don't recall the exact words—was that the exodus of the Jews from Egypt (and I can pretty much assume that he did not use the word "exodus") harmed Egypt's potential economic growth. "The Jews," as Mubarak put it, "always contributed to the well-being of the nation, and without them, it became more difficult for Egypt to grow."

I found the comment reassuring. It conveyed the sense that though Egypt's president might have real issues with Israel, he was not an anti-Semite. An Egyptian president admitting to, and lamenting, anti-Semitic actions taken by an earlier Egyptian leader—and one as revered as Nasser—had to be viewed as a major step forward.

And I must admit I was also pretty pleased when he spoke, in his heavily accented English, of Yasser Arafat somewhat critically: "Arafat operates by committee and he isn't brave in making painful decisions."

But then, Mubarak went on to insist that Arafat was basically a good person, and sincerely committed to creating a homeland for his people. When we pressed him as to why Arafat was so opposed to reaching any peace agreement with Israel—which was the Palestinians' only hope to bring about some sort of national homeland—Mubarak threw out an intriguing response: "Arafat's comments are for public consumption only."

What became apparent at that first meeting, and even more so at future meetings with the Egyptian president, was that he really wanted us to help bring about a renewed U.S. interest in the area, ideally culminating in a peace conference involving Israel, the Arab countries, and the Palestinians. Egypt, obviously, was the Arab country most anxious for a peace agreement between Israel and her neighbors, since that would be the best hope to end Egypt's isolation in the Arab world. But now, to Mubarak's extraordinary frustration, instead of an openness to peace developing between Israel and her neighbors, the situation was getting worse. Inside Israel, the Palestinian Intifada (1987–1993) had erupted, and every night, throughout the Middle East, viewers watched television clips of stone-throwing Palestinian protestors, many of them barely more than children, being shot at, and severely hurt, by rubber bullets fired by Israeli soldiers. Aside from the hatred against Israel such scenes provoked, they hardly increased affection for Egypt, the only Arab country to make peace with Israel.

What Mubarak wanted was some gesture by Israel, some reaching out to the Palestinians. Instead, all he, and the rest of the Arab world, believed they were getting from Israeli prime minister Yitzhak Shamir was a digging in of heels and intransigence. Knowing full well my background and sympathies—and knowing that Wayne was sympathetic to Israel as well—Mubarak told us that "the time is now for peace and that peace is within their grasp. Can the Israeli Prime Minister not see that the moment for peace is now?"

The longer we spoke, the more Mubarak's low regard for Shamir became apparent: "Shamir has no courage. He is terrified of [Ariel] Sharon." As Mubarak understood it, Shamir was terrified that if he made any gesture of moderation, the highly popular and influential Sharon would thrust him out as head of the Likud Party.

Meanwhile, while Shamir was doing nothing, the attempts of American secretary of state George Shultz to bring about a break in the Israeli/Palestinian deadlock were floundering. Shultz and his team at the State Department had drafted a framework for a peace process that would depend on what the secretary of state called an "interlock," a fixed timetable would be set so a Palestinian interim government would be the first step to final status negotiations, likely ending in a Jordanian/Palestinian confederation. Then, once the Palestinian issue was dealt with and resolved, the way would be paved for peaceful relations between Israel and all her neighbors based on UN Security Council Resolution 242, with its "land for peace" formula.

During a visit by Shultz to the area in March 1988, a draft of the framework for negotiations had been given to Arab and Israeli leaders alike. But, Mubarak noted bitterly, Shamir was not picking up on it; he wasn't flat out rejecting it he couldn't so flagrantly ignore an American request—but his strategy seemed to be to ignore discussing the proposal and just hope that it would die.

Indeed, one aspect of Shultz's document had already become the focus of much attention: his call for an international conference to mark the beginning of a renewed peace process. This idea, it was now apparent, particularly entranced Mubarak; he spoke of such a conference as "a golden opportunity."

On the other hand, it was widely known that Shamir, believing that such a conference would lead to unfair and destructive pressure on Israel, was determined to make sure it didn't happen. Indeed, when Shamir visited Washington a few weeks earlier, he had tried to resist President Reagan's urgings to participate in such a gathering. The president's pressure had not been subtle: "Those who will say 'no' to the United States plan...need not answer to the United States. They'll need to answer to their people on why they turned down a realistic and sensible plan to achieve negotiations." Shamir had somewhat lamely responded, "I have strong reservations concerning the proposed international conference which, in my view, is not conducive to peace," and later told concerned pro-Israel supporters, "Sometimes there are differences between the best of friends." It was now clear that because of Reagan's strong pressure, Israel could not fully resist America's urging to participate in the conference, but there was also no question that Shamir would do all he could to limit the damage he feared this conclave could cause Israel.

It was a heady experience for me, this first meeting with a major Arab leader. I was certainly happy to hear Mubarak express his openness to peace with Israel, and even to hear of his ambivalence toward Arafat. It was not what my years of involvement in Jewish political life had prepared me to expect.

But the truth is, the most important insight I gained that day—and it was not a happy one—came not from President Mubarak, but from Dr. Osama El-Baz, who was, in effect, Mubarak's national security advisor. A Harvard Law School graduate, El-Baz was an elegant, soft-spoken man of deeply held convictions who had helped broker the 1979 peace treaty with Israel. Indeed, he had been the most militant Egyptian representative in those negotiations, and in Jimmy Carter's account of the Camp David negotiations, he wrote that he knew that if he could convince El-Baz on a given point, that Sadat and the rest of the Egyptian negotiating team would come around.

I was shocked, therefore, that this enormously sophisticated man, whose behavior toward us was at all times respectful and courteous, seemed to hold the most frightfully inaccurate views about Israel. Notions that El-Baz regarded as self-evident truths struck me as paranoid. For example, at one point—directing his comments to me— he said, "Israel is an expansionist country. Look at their flag. It's a Star of David between two blue lines. Those two lines represent the Nile and Euphrates." In other words, the Israeli flag itself symbolized Israel's desire to dominate the Middle East, from Egypt to Iraq.

I couldn't believe that he was serious. "Come on," I said, "you're kidding. Israel has no such expansionist ideas."

"Well then, why don't they draw their borders?"

This was the first time I had ever heard such a question, but with the passage of time, I stopped regarding it as either paranoid or ludicrous (the misconceptions about the Israeli flag, which are widespread, are indeed paranoiac and ludicrous). As Arab leader after Arab leader told me, "We don't have anything against Israel's existence, but we have something against Israel's intentions," I started to understand that the Arab fear of Israel as an expansionist state was not a propaganda ploy, but very real. Mubarak too would regularly raise this issue: "Why doesn't Israel declare its borders?"

The combined effect of Israel having the strongest army in the Middle East and not setting down exact borders really concerned and frightened them. The Arabs had fought wars with Israel in 1948, 1956, 1967, and 1973, and at the end of the first three wars Israel was bigger than it had been before the conflict. Now I, a product of a Zionist upbringing and commitment, never regarded this as strange or as evidence of bad intentions on Israel's part. Instead of blaming Israel, the Arab world, I had always felt, should blame itself. If the Arabs had simply accepted Israel's existence, and had neither invaded (as they had done in 1948), or threatened Israel (as they had done in

1967), none of Israel's territorial gains would have come about. Israel's occupation of the Sinai desert in 1967 had not come about because of an expansionist dream, but because Egypt's President Nasser had threatened to destroy her, and had, in violation of international agreements, closed the Strait of Tiran to Israeli ships and to foreign ships carrying strategic materials to Israel. Under international law, such an attempt at economic strangulation constituted a casus belli, legal grounds to go to war.* But still Israel did not do so until after Nasser started making pronouncements such as, "Our basic objective will be the destruction of Israel." Then, once Israel occupied the Sinai, what was she supposed to do? Return it to the very people who said they would use it as a launching pad to foment future attacks against her? Indeed, as El-Baz himself knew, once Egypt signaled its willingness to make peace, Israel returned every inch of the land she had conquered.

But now, despite my skeptical thoughts, for the first time in my life I started to understand the conflict from another perspective. Over the coming years, Osama El-Baz became a close friend to Wayne and I, and, invariably, he was among those whom we consulted before we would meet with President Mubarak—and with other Arab leaders such as Syrian president Hafez Assad—and we would raise with him the issues we intended to discuss. I

---

* As Abba Eban declared in a speech at the UN shortly after the end of the Six-Day War: "From May 24 onward [the day Egypt closed the Strait of Tiran to Israel], the question of who started the war or who fired the first shot became momentously irrelevant. There is no difference in civil law between murdering a man by slow strangulation or killing him by a shot to the head." In addition, Nasser also evicted UN peacekeepers in the Sinai, and illegally moved in its troops.

still remember the question that El-Baz kept coming back to that morning: "Why doesn't Israel draw its borders and declare that these are their borders? I still believe that that is in Israel's best interest."

Another thing that stands out for me from that first trip is that I found myself liking the Egyptian people more than I had expected to. The truth is, I have always liked most people I meet, but I feared that, in Egypt, I would find myself continually running into narrow-minded religious extremists and anti-Israel fanatics. Instead, as I walked down the streets of Cairo, I was struck by how easy-going most of the people seemed.

I remember one incident; it was minor, but it made an impression. I saw a man carrying maybe eight bolts of textiles on his shoulders; another man bumped into him and all the textiles fell to the ground. It was just the sort of incident that could have triggered angry words, and maybe even a fight. Instead, the two men looked at each other, smiled, and even laughed a bit. Then the one who caused the accident helped the other pick up the bolts, and off they both went.

Cairo, as I soon came to recognize, might be poor— but that didn't diminish the sense of vitality, energy, and goodwill I felt from so many of the people. I suppose that was one of the things that made me feel that the some-what cold peace that already existed between Egypt and Israel could hold and one day expand into a really warm peace.

Something else struck me on that trip. It was some-thing I was familiar with from anti-Semitic propaganda: the belief that Jews had enormous political and economic power, and that they controlled and directed the des-tinies of nations. Nobody expressed this stereotype to me in quite so crude a manner, but it was clear that some of the Arab leaders to whom we spoke believed that the American-Jewish community had enormous power over the American political process. But the belief that American Jews were so powerful meant that it gave people like me—a fairly wealthy American Jewish businessman—an opportunity to discuss important issues with Arab leaders and to move them toward recognition of Israel. After all, if they regarded Jews as politically weak and insignificant, why would they meet with us?

By the time I left Egypt, I felt that the time had come for the American Jewish community to start exerting far more of whatever power it did possess to help further the peace process. It also occurred to me that it would be a good idea for there to be more trips like the one Wayne and I had taken. The impact of these visits, both on the Arab leaders and on the Jewish leaders, could be great.

A full half-year passed before we returned to Egypt (in December 1988), and this time we met with the leaders of the Islamist Labor Party, Egypt's opposition party. The party represented Islamic fundamentalists, including supporters of the organization known as the Muslim Brotherhood. Wayne and I met with Mamoun El-Hodeiby, the spiritual leader of the Muslim Brotherhood, and Ibrahim Shukry, a son of the party's founder. In theory, the Muslim Brotherhood was an outlawed organization, but the government permitted it to exist within the framework of the Labor Party. I had never had occasion to meet with Muslim fundamentalists before—and the phenomenon was less widely known in 1988 than it is today—and I found the encounter quite disturbing. Indeed, had Wayne and I met with these two men on our first trip to Egypt, instead of with President Mubarak and Osama El-Baz, we probably would have left Egypt despondent rather than optimistic about the prospects for peace.

El-Hodeiby and Shukry's rage was palpable, further inflamed by the fact that they were now face to face with an American Jewish businessman and an American congressman, the equivalent to them of the devil and his apprentice. Once again, we heard the charges leveled against the Israeli flag; this time we were told that the flag's two blue lines represented the Nile and Tigris rivers, both of which the Israelis intended to one day capture. After sharing this "insight" with us, El-Hodeiby turned to Wayne, about whom he had obviously been briefed, and said, "Most Muslims feel that the greatest crime of the twentieth century is the stealing away of the Palestinian homeland. The people of Utah would not tolerate it if the United Nations would come along and give most of its state to outsiders. This is the situation that has settled in the hearts of all people in the area." El-Hodeiby accused Israel not only of stealing the Palestinians' land, but also of treating the Palestinians under her rule as slave laborers.

Unlike the sense of civility that characterized our earlier meetings—a civility that existed even when President Mubarak or Dr. El-Baz expressed criticism of Israel—El-Hodeiby and Shukry related to us as if we were murderers or, at the very least, supporters of murderers. I realized then just how much blind rage infected some of the Arab populace, and that it was this rage that would pose a major obstacle to bringing about peace between Israel and her neighbors. Unfortunately, in the more than fifteen years since this meeting took place—and with the enormous spread of Islamic fundamentalism—this fury has increased, not diminished.

One of the worst effects of this rage is that it restrains more moderate and pragmatic Arab leaders from aggressively promoting peace with Israel. Men such as Mubarak are well aware of how much good can be accomplished by a large expansion of Israeli-Arab economic ties; just imagine the help that could be extended by Israeli agriculturalists to Egyptian farmers, help that would dramatically increase the quantity of food grown and harvested, and thereby raise the quality of lives and save lives. There is no question that Mubarak and many of the leading figures in the Arab world know what benefits a full peace with Israel will bring to their countries, but they also know that in the prevailing political climate it is dangerous to state such a truth.

What also struck me on this second trip—and perhaps I was naïve for not seeing this before—is the extent to which the Arab people truly perceive Israel as the aggressor in the Arab/Israel conflict. I always thought that the relentless depiction of Israel as the evil assailant was just propaganda, but that no one really believed it. After all, I knew—and didn't everybody else know as well?—that five Arab countries invaded Israel on the day it was founded, May 15, 1948. So how could Israel be labeled the aggressor in that war? And the same had happened again in 1973 (only this time it was just two countries, Egypt and Syria). Even in 1967, when Israel struck first, it was only because Egypt, Syria, and other Arab nations, including Iraq, had called for a war of extermination against her.

The Arab take on all this was, of course, very different. True, they would admit that Arab countries had invaded Israel in 1948, but only because they believed that the Jews had established a country on land stolen from the Palestinians. The Arab invasion, therefore, in their view, should not be viewed as aggression. Rather, from the Arab perspective, what happened in 1948 was an attempt by a law-abiding people to regain that which had been stolen from them. The Egyptian-Syrian attack against Israel in 1973 was motivated by the same urge; in this case, according to their view, to regain the land stolen from them by Israel in 1967. And as regards the 1967 War, the Arab world points out, Israel had struck the first blow, a surprise attack that destroyed the Egyptian and Syrian air forces.

What we were repeatedly encountering in Egypt, in other words, was the mirror image of what people felt in Israel. The Arabs believed that they were a peaceful people whose sovereignty and existence were threatened by Israel, just as the Israelis felt that they were a peaceful people whose sovereignty and existence were threatened by their surrounding Arab neighbors.

Wayne and I understood that we were not going to make any impact on the extremists on both sides of the political agenda. The Mamoun El-Hodeibys and Ibrahim Shukrys of the world were never going to believe that the Jewish people of Israel wanted to live in peace and had a right to do so, just as Meir Kahane and his followers—and later the Yigal Amirs—were never going to accept that Palestinians, too, like the Jews, had a right to a homeland.

What further inflamed the extremists on both sides—and this is yet another unhappy realization to which I came—is the tendency of people who want to deny basic rights to others to justify their behavior by claiming that it is not them, but the other side, that is motivated by enmity and hatred ("Oh, we Arabs have nothing against the Jews. But the Israelis hate Arabs and want to destroy us, or treat us as slaves." Or, "Israel offers Arabs who live here more rights than Arabs have in any other country. But still, the Arab world is dominated by people who want to murder all Israelis. So what choice do we have?

We have to defend ourselves"). *It became clear to me on that second trip, more than on the first, that our job was to help each side understand the other.*

But how could we do it? If millions of people think so badly of the other side, how do you go about trying to change their perception? I came back to a theory I had developed during long years of business negotiations. As I understand it, one person runs every company, one person runs every organization, and one person runs every country.* That one man or woman may have a lot of advisers—and a lot of other people might be working there—but only he or she runs things and makes all the important decisions. The key is to get to that person.

So if Wayne and I were going to make any progress in influencing the Arab world's perceptions of Israel (and vice versa), we were going to have to appeal to, and influence, the leaders of the Arab countries (and of Israel as well). If we could, for example, convince the leader of a particular country to move toward peace with Israel, it would only be a matter of time before other elements in the country's political system would fall into line. And even if some of the elements of a society didn't do so, some would and—at the very least—by convincing the country's leader, you'd have a powerful proponent of peace on your side. Thus, there might not be uniform support for peace in Egypt, but if you consider how differently Egypt has acted toward Israel under the leadership of Sadat and Mubarak than it did under Nasser, it becomes apparent that the attitude of the person in charge is the most significant influence on how the

---

* This is particularly true in nondemocratic societies, but it is true in democracies as well; the president is the person most influential in setting the country's agenda.

average person thinks. Under Nasser, with his frequent hysterical rantings against Israel, hundreds of thousands of Egyptians could be mobilized to take to the streets to demonstrate in support of war. Under Sadat and Mubarak, it has been clear that, even though many Egyptians believe that Israel has acted unjustly toward the Palestinians, few Egyptians want to send their sons to fight Israel. And if this state of affairs continues for another generation, with the country's leader advocating peace with Israel, the attitude of the average Egyptian toward Israel will very likely become even more positive.

So, despite our discouraging encounter with the two leaders of the Muslim Brotherhood, I still sensed that openness to peace was already in the air and, even more important, that it could not be stopped. The great French writer Victor Hugo used to say, "There is nothing so powerful as an idea whose time has come."

Much to our surprise, this feeling was reinforced on the same trip when we went to Saudi Arabia, a country where I expected to find no openness to Israel at all. Over the years, I had heard disturbing reports about Saudi Wahhabism, and the country's climate of religious extremism. Here again, Wayne's credentials as a congressman achieved remarkable results. We were hosted by Saudi King Fahd in his incredibly lavish guest palace. I still remember the glittering chandelier hanging down five stories from the palace's center. Wayne, myself, and his staff were given an entire wing of one floor. Wayne's suite alone had three bedrooms, and a dining room that could seat twenty guests. But what impressed me far more than the material extravagance was the moderate tone Saudi officials took when talking to us about Israel. Sure, they were bitter against Israel, but they spoke with a greater sense of balance and pragmatism than I had expected. As the deputy foreign minister, Sheik Abdul Rahman El-Mansuri, told us: "We are pushing for peace. Of course, it can't come overnight, but we need peace more than the Israelis. It's good for economic development and stability and that's what we want."

It would be nice to report that such sentiments were matched by tangible, concrete actions taken by the Saudis to demonstrate to Israel that they were serious about peace. It would also be nice to report that when we passed on this information to the Israelis they contacted the Saudis either directly or through the United States, and responded to this outright overture of peace. But in neither case did such actions occur.

But still I was encouraged. In the past, no Saudi foreign minister would have spoken to a congressman and a Jewish visitor about Israel in so moderate and civil a manner (there probably would have been few, if any, Jewish visitors allowed into the country).* This was a far cry from the 1950s, when Saudi Arabia's King Saud liked to declare, "Israeli is to the entire Arab world like a cancer to the human body, and the only way of remedy is to uproot it just like a cancer....We Arabs total about fifty million. Why don't we sacrifice ten million of our number and live in pride and self-respect?"† Even years later, the most heavy-handed anti-Semitism and anti-Zionism continued to endure. King Faisal used to present guests of his regime with copies of *The Protocols of the Elders of Zion*, an

---

* When Henry Kissinger visited Saudi Arabia several times in the 1970s, it was in his capacity as America's secretary of state, not as a Jewish leader.

† Given that Israel's entire population then was only about one million, the fact that King Saud thought that ten million Arabs would die in the attempt to destroy Israel shows that he saw Jews in superhuman physical terms.

anti-Semitic forgery that was used, by the Nazis among others, as a justification for genocide against the Jews. It was known to be one of Faisal's favorite books.

As was apparent to Wayne and me, the movement to change the Arab world's attitude and relationship to Israel was going to be slow-moving and subtle. Convinced as I was that the openness to change among the Arabs was real, I could also understand Israelis who doubted its sincerity. And yet, if there would be no Israeli response to these tentative openings from Arab leaders and diplomats, the Arab-Israeli conflict would just continue to escalate.

But, as I soon learned, there was one person in Israel who had foreseen—and who wanted to help bring about—change: Israel's immediate past prime minister, Shimon Peres.

When Wayne and I first met with him, Peres was serving as finance minister in a Labor-Likud unity government, headed by Yitzhak Shamir.* He soon became a close friend.

Peres is one of those fascinating figures whose involvement in Israel's political affairs has spanned the life of the country itself. In the 1950s, he played a key role in

---

* Americans tend to be dumbfounded when they hear something like this, since it is impossible to imagine an American ex-president serving in any cabinet position, let alone serving under a president of the opposite party. But Israel has a very different political system from that of the United States. As I shall have occasion to explain later, in some ways, Israel's electoral and proportional representation political system is more democratic in granting power to fringe and minority groups, but I also think that its electoral system makes it very difficult, if not impossible, to achieve an agreement with the Palestinians, even though that is what the large majority of Israelis want.

securing French arms for Israel's defense establishment. This was vital, since, in those days, the United States was not willing to sell arms to Israel. In 1985, as prime minister, Peres spearheaded Israel's withdrawal from Lebanon, and in 1987 he held secret negotiations with King Hussein.

Peres has a trait uncommon among politicians: he thinks with regards to long-term solutions, not just how to win the next election. I remember something Peres said to us on our first or second trip. At the time, as I noted, he was serving under Prime Minister Shamir, whose views on peace and on accommodation with the Arab world were uncompromising. Peres, a combination visionary and pragmatist, told us: "I am for peace. I am not going to move the prime minister. I am going to move the people. I am going for the things that are good for the country."

That statement epitomized Peres, who, for most of his years as a peace advocate, faced an uphill battle. The battle was continually made near-impossible, not only by Jewish opposition, but by Arab terrorism and violence. Recalling the last election he was a part of, he mentioned that when Arab terrorists blew up a bus and killed a woman and her three children, "I knew I lost the elections. It is a matter of emotion. Ninety percent of the problem is emotional."

Peres felt that what Jews and Arabs alike had to apply to their problems was a lot more reason and a lot less emotion. But there was no large-scale movement toward this in the Arab world, and the Israelis, embittered by the many wars and continuous terrorist attacks—and always conscious of the atrocities of the Holocaust—had developed a trench mentality.

What immediately attracted Wayne and me to Peres was that he had a tangible vision of how to get to peace. Also, he didn't speak in empty generalities; he knew what was required to change the atmosphere in the Middle East. As Peres saw it, the recently erupted Intifada had shaken up many Israelis, and while it increased hatred toward the Arabs, it had also caused many Israelis to question the viability of Israel's occupying another people. What an increasing number of Israelis were coming to understand was that whether or not a Palestinian people with a cohesive national identity had existed prior to 1948 was no longer a relevant question. Golda Meir could, as prime minister, still have gotten away with pronouncements such as, "There is no such thing as a Palestinian people." But the fact was that a Palestinian people with a national identity existed now, and they were not going away.

Of course—and this was part of Peres's uphill battle—many Israelis could not bear the thought of parting with any piece of the West Bank, home to Judaism's Patriarchs, and the territory in which so much of biblical history had occurred (notwithstanding that probably fewer than 1,500 Jews had lived in the West Bank prior to 1948). And even more Israelis could not swallow the possibility of permitting a new and hostile country to be established alongside them, next door to Jerusalem, and only miles away from Israel's financial center, and largest city, Tel Aviv.

Even then I understood that there was no argument that would make an impact on those Israelis who deemed it forbidden to give back any part of the biblical land of Israel. Such people, in their speeches and writings, might use Arab violence as an excuse for not establishing a

Palestinian state, but ultimately, even if the Palestinians turned into a nation of Gandhis, such Israelis would still oppose any territorial compromise.

As regards the other Israelis, the far larger group who opposed a Palestinian state because they feared it would become a launching pad for attacks against Israel, one had to acknowledge that they had good reasons for their fears.* They viewed territorial concessions as making Israel more vulnerable, not more secure. Indeed, to just denounce them as imperialists and occupiers, as the Left did, was unfair and wrong. The time had come, therefore, for the Palestinians to address the Israelis' legitimate fears. What was needed was an elimination of violence and of the threat of violence on the Arab side. As Peres said: "Arafat should go from a strategy of terror to a strategy of politics."

In addition to Peres's vision, what also drew us to him was something more chemical. As Wayne once put it, "He actually respects us. You go to Rabin and you feel like you are bothering him. You go to Shimon and you feel like he's listening to you." It was clear that Peres liked us, as we liked him, and, more important, that he believed that the two of us could play a useful function in the search for peace. Whenever we were in Israel, we would have long, talk-filled dinners with him.

On that second trip, in December 1988, we visited Palestinian refugee camps where, for the first time, I saw the effects the violence and the Israeli reaction to it were having on the people who lived in the West Bank. We saw the remains of homes that had been blown up by the Is-

---

* But, in reality, a border that was fortified and strong, and with a high wall, would be a better defense against West Bank terrorism than occupying the West Bank without a strong border.

raelis as punishment for a family member who had been involved in anti-Israeli terrorism. I understood why the Israelis had done this, to discourage such behavior, but still, the sight of a devastated, often elderly couple—who probably didn't know about their son's plan—standing alongside their destroyed house pained us.

I also remember being taken to a Palestinian hospital where we met many of the thirty-six people who had been injured in that day's scuffles and battles with the Israelis.

The building was a decrepit and unkempt concrete structure; it was overcrowded and understaffed, and there was little evidence that much attention was directed to maintaining proper sanitary conditions. The thought that anyone dear to me would be treated in such a facility horrified me.

We also saw five young men lying in bed, brain-dead; a mother was hovering over one of the boys pleading with him to return to consciousness. Most of these boys were the victims of the rubber bullets fired by Israeli troops into crowds of lethal stone-throwers. Scenes such as this, I knew, were being broadcast nightly throughout the Arab world.

As I looked at the tragedies going on inside that room, I felt sadness and frustration even more than anger. I could imagine the feelings and fright of the Israeli soldiers who had fired these bullets, themselves teenagers or a little older, surrounded by stone-throwing violent protestors. Of course, they felt endangered, and felt the need to protect themselves.

The enemy of the Israelis, I understood that day, was not the Palestinians, and the enemy of the Palestinians was not the Israelis. The enemy was the conflict itself. That's what had to end.

But it was not clear to me that Yitzhak Rabin, then Shamir's defense minister, felt the same way. When Wayne and I met with Rabin, he became agitated any time we voiced concern over the escalating violence. Rabin favored territorial compromise within the context of a peace settlement, but he saw no way to deal with the Intifada's violence other than with Israeli counterviolence. "Running away from violence only encourages more violence," he told us. It was Rabin's desire to limit the violence that had motivated him to instruct soldiers to fire rubber bullets instead of conventional ones, and to try in confrontations to stop violent protestors without having to kill them. But though Rabin desired to hold down Arab deaths, it was also clear to us that he had bound himself to a policy that was not working; rubber bullets and the breaking of arms and legs was not causing the Intifada to go away. If anything, it was getting worse.

The late Jewish theologian Rabbi Abraham Joshua Heschel used to tell a story about a group of inexperienced mountain climbers who, when a rocky ledge gave way beneath them, tumbled headlong into a deep pit. The climbers recovered from their horror only to find themselves set upon by a swarm of angry snakes. For each snake the desperate men killed, it seemed ten more sprung up to replace it. Strangely enough, one man seemed to stand apart from the fight. When his besieged companions angrily criticized him for not fighting, the man called back: "If we remain here, we shall be dead before the snakes. I am searching for a way of escape from the pit for all of us."

People on both sides of the Israeli-Palestinian conflict were fighting a never-ending supply of snakes that would, sooner or later, overwhelm them. We needed to find a way of escape from the pit for Israelis and Palestinians alike.

I often thought of my theory of the most effective way to bring about change: to reach the one man, the leader, the one who could make change happen. The Intifada, I understood, could only be halted from the top down. And there was only one man who could halt it. His name was Yasser Arafat and, after having been expelled from Lebanon, he was now living in Tunisia. It was there that we would have to go.

THREE

Arafat in Tunis

For a Jew like myself, a passionate Jew committed both to my religion and people, it was not an easy thing to meet with Yasser Arafat. The purpose of such a meeting, after all, is to achieve something positive, and if you act argumentatively, nothing positive will be achieved. So, at the very least, you have to speak politely, try to be warm, and hope that something of a friendship develops. But how comfortable would I be trying to develop a friendly relationship with a man accused of shedding so much Jewish blood? Yasser Arafat might have a litany of complaints a mile long against Israel, but none of them would justify actions he had ordered, such as the attack by PLO terrorists on a school in the Israeli city of Ma'alot, which led to the killing of twenty-five schoolchildren, or the attack on the Israeli athletes at the 1972 Munich Olympics, which led to the murder of eleven Israeli Olympians.

Nonetheless, as Yitzhak Rabin was later to remark, "You don't make peace with your friends." So if Wayne and I were not going to speak to Arafat in an effort to achieve a settlement of the Israeli-Palestinian conflict, with whom then would we speak?

Obviously, it was helpful to have meetings with men such as President Mubarak and Osama El-Baz, and with leaders throughout the Arab world. But they all made it clear that whatever settlements Israel might try to make with them would still not solve the most basic and intractable problem of all, the status of the Palestinians. Israel could try to negotiate peace agreements with its other Arab neighbors, but if it didn't negotiate one with the Palestinians, Israel would continue to be wracked by conflict and terrorism. Furthermore, although men such as President Mubarak, King Hussein of Jordan, and President Assad of Syria could make the argument on behalf of the Palestinians, they also emphasized that only one man, Arafat, could speak for the Palestinians. So if Wayne and I were serious about our quest for peace, we would have to meet with him.

The opportunity to meet Arafat had first presented itself to us less than two months earlier, during our December 1988 trip to Saudi Arabia. While we were there, Arafat unexpectedly flew into Riyadh to meet with the king. It was clear that something important was happening or was about to happen.

A short time earlier, Arafat had, for the first time, declared that all countries in the Middle East—he did not mention Israel by name—had a right to peace and security. His motivation for making this statement had less to do with goodwill toward Israel than with his desire to gain recognition from the United States. The Americans had imposed very specific conditions on him: He would have to publicly announce his acceptance of the Jewish state and its right to exist, and he would have to categorically renounce support for terrorism. Arafat's trial balloon, his declaration that all countries in the Middle East had a right to peace and security, was not sufficient to prompt the U.S. State Department to open a dialogue with the PLO. Indeed, a short time later, when Arafat asked for a visa to the United States so that he could say the "magic words" at the United Nations, Secretary of State Shultz denied him entry; he would still not be permitted into the United States.

Without recognition by the United States, Arafat feared he would become marginalized, and face declining relevance to the events, such as the Intifada, taking place in the West Bank and Gaza. So Arafat knew that he would have to utter the "magic words" soon.

We later learned that Arafat had now come to Saudi Arabia to consult with King Fahd. He was set to fly from Saudi Arabia to Geneva, and since Fahd was a major financial backer, he did not wish to alienate him. Arafat, therefore, wished to secure the king's blessings for the course he was about to take.

It turned out that on the second night of our stay at the king's palace, Arafat and his entourage were the only other guests there. Several Saudi officials approached us and asked if we would like to meet with him. But since Arafat was still regarded as a terrorist by the U.S. government, Wayne, who was a congressman, turned down the invitation.

That evening, we dined with Prince Abdullah, along with other prominent Saudis, at the Sab'a Restaurant. Fabric was draped along the walls to make the gourmet restaurant seem as if it were a giant tent. The dinner it-self was held in traditional Saudi style, with the men leaning on pillows, while reclining on the intricately pat-terned carpets. This scene put me in mind of the traditional Passover Seder in which participants are in-structed to lean on pillows to symbolize that they are free people; for one night a year, even the poorest Jew is sup-posed to recline like a free man of leisure. This dinner though was a lot more lavish than any Passover Seder I had attended. I remember that some forty dishes were set in front of us.

A major topic of conversation that night was Arafat's earlier meeting with the king. One of the princes said to me: "Do you know that Arafat has agreed with the secre-tary of state to make a pronouncement recognizing Israel and disavowing terror?"

I questioned him about the matter further, and he told me with certainty that Arafat was going to do it. But I had trouble believing it. The PLO had for so long been wedded to Israel's destruction that I couldn't imagine him disavowing it, and renouncing terror. Even so, I thought that I must find a way to get this report to the Is-raelis. Arafat was obviously intending to say something new, and Israel should be ready with a reaction.

But how could I reach Israel and to whom should I speak? There were no phone lines between Israel and Saudi Arabia, and because the Saudis did not recognize Is-rael, communication between the two countries was forbidden. So, instead, I placed a call to Dan Rodgers, who was president of Thompson Medical, my company in the United States. Because I was speaking from a line in the guest palace I had little doubt that Saudi intelligence was listening in. I told Dan about the substance of what I had heard, and asked him to call Yitzhak Herzog (my lawyer in Israel, and a son of Chaim Herzog, Israel's former president) and pass on what I had told him. Herzog, I later learned, conveyed the message to Nimrod Novik, Shimon Peres's assistant. To this day, I don't know if the message ever got to Prime Minister Shamir, but I'm sure it wouldn't have mattered anyway. Shamir had already made it known that anything Arafat would say would "change nothing in our country or the territories."

It turned out of course that the prince was right and I was wrong. Speaking the following day in Geneva, in front of a specially convened UN assembly, Arafat said: "It [the Palestinian National Council] has also reaffirmed its rejection of terrorism, its rejection of terrorism in all its forms...." In addition, he announced the PLO's acceptance of "the right of all parties concerned in the Middle East conflict to exist in peace and security."

Obviously, Arafat had not mentioned Israel by name, and I admit that I would have been a lot happier had he done so. All he would have had to do was acknowledge the PLO's acceptance of "the right of all parties, including Israel...." But I also realized that Arafat had gone much further in his acceptance of Israel than anyone would have predicted even just a few months earlier.

Prime Minister Shamir was not impressed. As he announced in his response to Arafat's statement: "We're witnesses to the PLO's monumental act of deception....We are not ready and will never be ready to talk to the PLO." He then went on to express his hope that the United States would not be taken in by Arafat's words and would "never create any official contact with the PLO."

The United States still insisted on more precise guarantees from Arafat and the PLO, but also made clear that it would enter into a more substantive relationship with Arafat once it got them. And, in truth, when Secretary Shultz announced what the conditions were, Arafat accepted them within days—on December 13, to be precise. Arafat publicly declared his acceptance of UN Resolution 181, the 1947 resolution calling for the partition of Palestine into a Jewish and Arab state, and of Resolutions 242 and 338 (the "land for peace" resolutions) as the basis for negotiations with Israel—and here he spoke of Israel by name—within the framework of an international conference. At a press conference following his UN speech, Arafat repeated that "we totally and absolutely renounce all forms of terrorism," and then went on to note that it was not within his power, or within the power of any individual, to stop the Intifada. "The Intifada will come to an end only and only when practical and tangible steps have been taken toward achievement of our national aims and the establishment of our independent Palestinian state."

In return, and I imagine to Prime Minister Shamir's immense dissatisfaction, Secretary of State Shultz responded: "The Palestine Liberation Organization today issued a statement in which it accepted UN Security Council Resolutions 242 and 338, recognized Israel's right to exist in peace and security, and renounced terrorism. As a result, the United States is prepared for a substantive dialogue with PLO representatives." Shultz then designated Robert Pelletreau American ambassador to Tunisia, where Arafat was residing, as the only authorized channel for this dialogue. He went on to express the hope that this would help bring about a comprehensive peace in the Middle East, and represent a step "toward the beginning of direct negotiations between the parties, which alone can lead to such a peace."

After Arafat made his statement, Wayne and I started regretting that we had passed up the opportunity to meet with him in Saudi Arabia. It was clear to both of us now that something even more substantial than we had earlier realized had changed in the Middle East. At least some of the Arab nations, we already knew, were ready to turn a new leaf in their relations with Israel. But ultimately, any peace between Israel and the Arab world depended on a solution to the Palestinian problem. In that regard, nothing had changed. Sadat himself had said it in his historic speech to the Israeli Knesset on November 20, 1977: "As for the Palestine cause, nobody can deny that it is the crux of the entire problem...and so long as it continues to be unresolved, the conflict will continue to aggravate, reaching new dimensions."

More than ten years had passed since Sadat had made this pronouncement, and every word in it had been prophetic.

A few weeks later, after we returned to the United States, Wayne went to see Prince Bandar, the Saudi ambassador to the United States, and expressed his regret about not meeting with Arafat when we had the chance. Bandar said he'd arrange a meeting for the two of us.

Wayne and I knew that we would be among the first Americans to meet with Arafat after the U.S. recognition, and Representative Lee Hamilton, the chairman of the House Middle East Sub-Committee, encouraged Wayne to make the visit, but warned him that he'd get flack from the American Jewish community.

A lot of congressmen at the time still regarded a visit to Arafat as anathema, and it was not only because of his terrorist acts against Israel. Arafat had American blood on his hands as well, having given the order to murder Cleo Noel, Jr., America's ambassador to the Sudan in 1973, along with the charge d'affaires of the American and Belgian embassies.*

Wayne and I both believed Arafat had done some terrible things. But we were meeting with him for one reason, and for one reason only. He was the head of the PLO, the organization regarded as the central institution by most Palestinians. Much as we abhorred things he and the PLO had done, he was considered the only legitimate leader of the Palestinians and, consequently, the only one with whom we could have a meaningful and potentially significant conversation.

After speaking to Bandar and Hamilton, Wayne called me: "What do you think, should we go?"

---

* On March 1, 1973, a gang of eight operatives of the Black September Organization stormed a party at the Saudi Arabian embassy in Khartoum. The party had been held in honor of the imminent departure of George Curtis Moore, the American charge d'affaires at the United States embassy in Khartoum. The Black September gang took Moore and two others hostage—Cleo Noel, Jr., the U.S. ambassador to Sudan, and Guy Eid, the Belgian embassy's charge d'affaires (two other diplomats who had been taken were released). The Black September terrorists demanded the release of Sirhan Sirhan, Robert Kennedy's assassin, the release of a Black September leader held in Jordan, and the release of several members of the Baader-Meinhof gang in Germany. On March 2, President Nixon and representatives of Jordan and Germany announced that they would not negotiate with the terrorists for the release of the diplomats. That evening, the Black September operatives, operating under the instructions of Arafat, marched Noel, Moore, and Eid to the embassy basement and brutally murdered them.

"Of course," I told him. "Just tell me when and where."

My instinct was to keep the news of the visit a secret. Wayne did consult with Congressman Tom Lantos of California. Lantos is an unusual figure; most notably, he is the only Holocaust survivor to serve in Congress. Lantos also had played a sort of mentoring role in Wayne's political life, and later even helped Wayne raise money when he was running (unsuccessfully) for the Senate. But when Wayne confided to Lantos what we were intending to do, Lantos grew very upset: "Oh, God, no. You can't do that. You'll kill yourself. He [Arafat] is a terrible person. He's a terrorist. He can't change."

Another congressman, Mel Levine, and then a man from the State Department, likewise, tried to discourage Wayne from making the trip. Ironically, the man from the State Department was Dennis Ross, who, a few years later, became the chief mediator in the negotiations between Israel and its neighbors, and went on to have many, many meetings with Arafat.

The discouragement we were getting was a bit unnerving. I also was not unconscious of the fact that the three people who opposed our going—Lantos, Levine, and Ross—were all Jews. Wayne and I went back and forth over this for about three or four days, and finally we just crossed our fingers and said, "What the hell, let's go." So Wayne called Prince Bandar and Bandar soon got back to him. Chairman Arafat would be pleased to receive us in ten days in Tunis.

I still recall my feelings at the time. I was excited, I was going to have a chance to find out what Arafat was all about, what kind of person he really was. And knowing that might enable Wayne and me to do something tangible to help bring peace between Israel and its neighbors.

Obviously, that would be the best-case scenario, but even if things didn't work out, I was sure the trip would prove to be, if nothing else, a true adventure.

On February 9, 1989, we flew to Tunisia. Robert Pellatreau, the American ambassador there—who had been apprised of our mission by the State Department—offered us two rooms in his home in which to prepare for what we knew would be a complex series of meetings. But then, on the very day of our arrival, tragedy struck within Arafat's family. His brother, the director of the Red Crescent (the Arab equivalent of the Red Cross) in Cairo, died of a sudden heart attack. Even as we were flying in, Arafat was already en route to Cairo for the funeral. Not certain when Arafat would return—at first, we were told he would be back in two days, but before we knew it four days had passed—we filled our days with briefings with the ambassador, while our evenings were spent in meetings with some of Arafat's deputies. One of them was Abu Mazen, who, fourteen years later, would become the first Palestinian prime minister. We met as well with Yasser Abed Rabbo, and Bassam Boshawri.

But our real desire, and the reason we had come to Tunis, was to meet with Arafat himself. He was now sending more moderate signals to the West, but we both felt that his intentions wouldn't be clear to us until we met him face-to-face. Even then, we knew, he could fool us, but we needed to get our own personal read on the man.

The one thing we knew for sure about Arafat is that he was a troublemaker, and seemingly always had been. In 1946, while he was a student at Cairo University, he was already smuggling arms into Palestine, then under the British Mandate, for the Arab cause. 1965 found him launching guerrilla raids into Israel from Jordan. He took over the PLO shortly after the 1967 War and by 1970, his troops posed such a threat to Jordan that that September—a month that the PLO came to call Black September—King Hussein's army went to war against the PLO and expelled them from Jordan (killing at least 1,200, and perhaps as many as 2,500 Palestinians). Arafat then ended up in Lebanon, where his forces regularly conducted assaults on Israel, and ultimately provoked Israel's retaliatory invasion of Lebanon. From there, he was evicted to Tunis.

Arafat's most famous public moment occurred at his 1974 appearance at the United Nations, in which he stepped to the lectern wearing his traditional keffiyah, fatigues, and a pistol—could one think of a more inappropriate way to enter the UN?—and said, in a manner both conciliatory and threatening, "I have come bearing an olive branch and a freedom fighter's gun. Do not let the olive branch fall from my hand."

With his recent renunciation of terror, we had to figure out two things. Was Arafat sincere? And if he was, would he be capable of shifting gears, from his lifelong role as terror boss to politician? We were hoping that a face-to-face meeting would enable us to intuit that.

I remember that Wayne arrived in Tunis with pages and pages of prepared questions, fifty or more of them. The funny thing was, we both sensed that Ambassador Pelletreau was somewhat jealous of us. He hadn't yet been cleared by the State Department to speak to Arafat himself, so we, in effect, became his subordinates. Pelletreau's questions, based on far more years of study of the Middle East than Wayne and I possessed, were more probing than ours.

After each meeting we had with Arafat's subordinates and later with Arafat himself, Pelletreau would debrief us at length, drawing out from us whatever details we could recall, and our impressions. All this material went straight into State Department files.

Finally, on our fourth night in Tunis, we received a phone call at about 8:00 P.M. The voice on the phone did not identify himself, nor did he tell us where we were heading. We were simply informed that a car would pick us up at the embassy. An hour later, two cars arrived. We entered one; the other, we could see, was filled with armed guards. At that time, Arafat used to sleep in a different safehouse every night. So the driver of our vehicle was not told where to go until we were both in the car.

I suppose Arafat could have chosen to change the location of our meeting at the last second. But as it was, we were taken to one of the PLO compounds in Tunis. It was heavily guarded by troops armed with machine guns and rifles. As we drove through the gates of the compound, we could see Arafat standing in his army uniform, his easily recognizable headdress, and carrying his pistol. As is common in Arab culture, he was waiting outside the front door to greet us, and the greeting he extended to us was effusive. Then we all entered the compound to dine.

While we were eating, Arafat delivered a long monologue on what it felt like to live without a country. The whole thrust of his speech was to present himself as a beleaguered man living—as all Palestinians were—as a wandering man without a passport and without an address, with nothing. It was this condition that drove him to make sure that the Palestinians would not continue to be people without a homeland, without a country.

Arafat's tone with us that night was a pleading one, quite unlike the man who had declared at the UN: "Do not let the olive branch fall from my hand." All he wanted now was independence for the Palestinians, and no more war with Israel. At one point, he even said, "I will take a Palestinian state in Jericho if I have to, if that's all I can get."

What Arafat was telling us was so at variance with his public persona that I was afraid people would think I had been hoodwinked, or was simply making things up. So midway through the meeting, I took out a little tape recorder and asked if I could record what he was saying. Wayne was afraid that Arafat might be upset, but he said, "No problem." In fact, he instructed his secretary to bring out a tape recorder as well, a gesture of mutuality.

Once we were on tape, I figured that this was the time for the two of us to push Arafat, to figure out what the red lines were in his negotiations with Israel. Wayne asked him if he was willing to accept a demilitarized zone; in other words, Palestinian autonomy on the West Bank or Gaza without a standing army, or advanced weapons.

Arafat did not dismiss Wayne's question out of hand, but he didn't accept its premise, either. All he said was that "This has to be on the agenda. But we are asking for our security, too. Everything has to be put on the table. They [the Israelis] have to understand our fears. And we have to understand their fears."

We asked him how he envisioned the negotiations with Israel proceeding, and what he would be pressing for.

"We are looking to have two states....Everything has to be put on the table—borders, security, settlements, refugees, sources of water, everything....We don't want to make a truce. We want a settlement, a full, lasting, comprehensive settlement." He kept reiterating that what the PLO was pushing now was a two-state solution. As he put it, "Our strategic line is to live and let live." He acknowledged that the PLO charter had called for one state, with Jews and Arabs living together. "Okay, they [the Israelis] don't want this. They want their own state—a Jewish state. We want our state. Two states. We [have] moved from a unitary solution to a two-state solution."

Arafat didn't want to pin down what the borders of that state would be—reminiscent of the Israeli refusal to do so. He just emphasized again and again that everything had to be put on the table. And he told us to tell Rabin and Peres—he didn't mention Shamir—that he didn't want this done piecemeal. "Without a package deal, nothing can be done." Once a two-state solution was agreed to in principle by the Israelis, then Arafat envisaged a step-by-step approach to all the issues, followed by a final agreement, and a program for implementation. At one point, Arafat said, "I don't want an army. Who am I going to fight—Israel? They're stronger than I am."

But, Arafat warned, without an advance Israeli acceptance of a two-state solution, "we will have what Shamir is saying, Judea and Samaria." In other words, as one of Arafat's advisers chimed in, the Palestinians need to know in advance that their central demand, a Palestinian state, would be met.

When I came back to my room, I made a note to myself: "It was one of the most exciting dinners that I have ever attended. The exchange of ideas was total. Everyone expressed their most honest and deepest feelings about the peace initiative and about the PLO's new role towards peace in the Middle East. Nobody underestimated the difficulty of moving towards peace between Israel, the Palestinians, and the Arab nations. But, on the other hand, no one expressed anything but a belief that there would be ultimate success because any other option is unacceptable."

I remembered something I had heard from Ali Maher, the Egyptian ambassador to Tunis. Maher saw the problem less as one of Israel and the Arabs, and more of one of moderates and extremists. "Our job," he said, "is to get the moderates together." If Arafat could be believed, it seemed that he was ready to join the camp of the moderates.

When we returned to the United States, we learned that our meeting, which was supposed to be kept secret, had been leaked to the press. I suppose there is a limit to what a congressman can do secretly, particularly when meeting with as prominent and controversial a figure as Arafat. Anyway, when Wayne arrived in Salt Lake City, he was met by members of the press who asked him if it was true that he had met with Arafat. Wayne was not the sort to lie, and he acknowledged that it was correct, and made it clear that he thought Arafat was sincere in his desire for peace. Then, for good measure, he mentioned my name as his traveling companion and, as you can imagine, that didn't go over too well in the Jewish community.

In truth, though, I took less flack than I expected. Sure, people started to kibitz me, but the criticisms by and large seemed restrained. I suppose our meeting, coming as it did *after* Arafat had made conciliatory statements, did not provoke as much wrath as it would have a year earlier. Still and all, even the people we knew in Israel's Labor Party were surprised at our reaction to Arafat, our belief that he was sincere in his desire for peace with Israel. The first Intifada was still at its height, and the general thinking in Israel was that Arafat was interested in peace only so that he could get a foothold in the region and then move to wipe out the rest of Israel.

I, in contrast, felt very good about the meeting, and about the relationships Wayne and I had forged. Here we were, an American congressman and an American businessman, and we were meeting with the people in the area who could make the decisions that could transform the climate from one of war to one of peace, from a rejection of Israel's very existence to an acceptance of Israel's right to exist as a sovereign Jewish state. Israel would have to make some serious territorial compromises on the West Bank for this to happen. But even so, how could I not be excited? There was a chance for peace. Jewish tradition has more prayers for peace than for anything else. But even as one recites those prayers daily, you always have the feeling that what you are praying for is peace in the future, most likely the distant future. But the peace we were hoping for seemed like it could happen soon.

I had lived in Israel for six years (from 1972 to 1978), and in all that time I wonder if there was a single day when there was not at least one article, and usually more, on the front page of the newspapers about the conflict with the Arabs and the military threats to Israel. Every parent with a child in the army—and in Israel there is a universal draft and little draft evasion—walked around in a state of continuous anxiety. But now, it was possible for me to envision that all this could come to an end. Indeed, how could I not be exhilarated?

FOUR

From the Madrid Conference to the Oslo Accords

When George Bush the father, that is, George H. W. Bush, became president in January 1989, he had more experience in foreign affairs than almost any American president who preceded him. Bush had directed the CIA, served as chief of the U.S. Liaison office in China, and as ambassador to the UN. In addition, of course, he had just finished serving as Ronald Reagan's vice-president for eight years. But for all of Bush's extensive background, it was hard to know exactly where he came down on the Arab-Israeli front. It was not an issue that he had dealt with or talked about much, nor was he known to have strong positions on it. The general perception of Bush was that he was a pragmatist.

The man Bush appointed as secretary of state, James Baker, was not known as a visionary either, but rather as a quick study and a dealmaker. It soon became clear that

3 1911 00508 9520

HICKSVILLE PUBLIC LIBRARY
169 JERUSALEM AVENUE
HICKSVILLE, NY 11801

the two of them intended to start their Middle East policy in a low-key manner, by trying to develop confidence-building measures. They, therefore, had no intention, certainly in Bush's first months in office, of fast-tracking a summit meeting and compelling reluctant nations, such as Israel and Syria, to participate. What Bush and Baker seemed to feel—and their attitude was reflected in an influential pamphlet entitled *Building for Peace**—was that the Arab-Israel conflict was not yet ripe for resolution. Therefore, premature activity by the United States—such as convening a high-profile conference or exerting strong pressure on Israel—would only undermine the goal of achieving peace in the region. In addition, a flurry of diplomatic activity might also magnify Arab expectations about the United States' political influence on Israel, and these unrealistic expectations might then lead to disappointment and resentment.

But on May 22, 1990, Secretary of State Baker issued the first indication that U.S. policy might start to exert more pressure on Israel. And if Baker intended to create a stir, he certainly picked the right forum at which to send forth his signal—the national AIPAC convention in Washington. As he declared to his audience's dismay: "Now is the time to lay aside once and for all the unrealistic vision of a greater Israel. Israeli interests in the West Bank and Gaza—security and otherwise—can be accommodated in a settlement based on Resolution 242. Forswear annexation. Stop settlement activity. Reach out

---

* The pamphlet was written by the Washington Institute for Near East Policy, and was widely acknowledged in the press as having had significant sway on both Bush and Baker.

to the Palestinians as neighbors who deserve political rights."*

Baker's comments about "the unrealistic vision of a greater Israel," and his demand to "Forswear annexation," made me wonder if he had been hearing the same complaint from Arab leaders that Wayne and I had long been hearing. As El-Baz had put it during that first meeting in Cairo: "Why doesn't Israel draw its borders, and declare that these are their borders?

Unfortunately, though, the situation was a lot less encouraging than when Wayne and I first met Arafat in Tunis more than a year earlier. Most significantly, the PLO had not completely foregone terrorism. In late May 1990, Israeli naval forces intercepted two heavily armed boatloads of Palestinians heading toward Tel Aviv, intending to attack Israeli civilians on the beachfront. Responsibility for the attempted raid was claimed by the Palestine Liberation Front, a radical offshoot of the PLO based in Baghdad. Arafat, while denying that the PLO was responsible for the intended attack, also refused to condemn it. Of equal concern, Arafat was increasingly allying himself with Saddam Hussein, the tyrannical ruler of Iraq, and a man who was stirring up anti-American fervor in his own country, in Jordan, and among the Palestinians. Saddam Hussein was presenting himself as the great exponent of Arab nationalism, an ideology that had suffered greatly since the 1967 War, and an ideology that Arafat, a secularist, had been drawn to since his youth.

---

* That same week, Baker testified before a congressional committee that "Settlements are the biggest obstacle to peace," and should be dismantled.

Arafat's refusal to renounce the terrorist attack outraged the White House. As Secretary of State Baker was later to observe: "Arafat had squandered any chance of establishing his credibility or even a scintilla of moral authority by refusing to renounce the terrorist attack."* On June 20 President Bush suspended the U.S. dialogue with the PLO.

Then, two months later, Saddam Hussein invaded Kuwait and, within days, announced Iraqi annexation of the country—acts of blatant aggression. In retrospect, I can only imagine that Hussein reasoned to himself as follows: "I have little to lose and a great deal to gain. The United States might issue denunciations, but there is no way it will react militarily to the invasion, and I will gain control of oil-rich Kuwait."

But, of course, Saddam Hussein had reasoned incorrectly, and on January 16, 1991, the U.S. coalition forces, operating under the auspices of the United Nations, and with the unprecedented support of the leading nations in the Arab world, went to war against Iraq. It quickly became clear that Iraq could not hold out very long, and in the hopes of turning the Arab world against the American-led coalition, Hussein started to rain down SCUD missiles on Israel. Hussein's hope was that attacking Israel would turn him into a hero among Arabs and might provoke Israel to attack Iraq. Once Israel did so, how could Arab countries such as Egypt, Saudi Arabia, and Syria continue to support an American-led war supported by Israel against a fellow Arab country?

But Israel, at the explicit request of the United States, did not retaliate. Her decision not to do so was a

---

* James A. Baker, III, *The Politics of Diplomacy* (New York: Putnam), page 130.

hard one for the proud and endangered Israelis to make. The decision was made easier by two factors, one of which seemed almost supernatural. Although the Iraqis rained down some thirty-nine SCUDs on Israel, only one person was directly killed in these attacks; others were injured, but few of them seriously.* Wayne, who was in Israel at the time, was convinced that "it is nothing short of a miracle. I visited three sites where SCUDs had hit; one of them had blown up four houses and destroyed fifty apartments, and no one was killed." The second reason was of course the extraordinary commitment the United States made to Israel; to place America's brand-new Patriot anti-missile system in the fields around Tel Aviv. These missiles were intended to knock Saddam's missiles out of the sky. While the Patriots didn't achieve their aim, the presence of the Patriots provided the Israelis with a psychological boost. The placing of the American anti-missile system preserved America's interest, which was in keeping Israel out of the coalition; if Israel was a part of it, the Arab participants would feel compelled to withdraw.

The success of the anti-Iraq coalition—the fact that the United States had been able to forge an alliance with the normally anti-American Syria, while drawing in Egypt and Saudi Arabia—left President Bush and his advisors convinced that there would be new opportunities in the post–Gulf War era. Meanwhile, the Palestinians and Jordan, who had both thrown their support to Saddam Hussein, were looking for opportunities to get into better graces with the West and with the rest of the Arab

---

* An additional four people met horrifying deaths by suffocating from their gas masks, and several others, it is not sure how many, died from heart attacks.

world. The PLO had lost much of its Saudi funding, and Kuwait retaliated against the PLO's support for Hussein by expelling all the Palestinians in its borders.

In the period following the victory over Iraq, Bush and his diplomats moved quickly. Bush himself set the agenda in a speech he gave before the U.N. General Assembly: "In the aftermath of Iraq's unconditional departure from Kuwait, I truly believe there may be opportunities for Iraq and Kuwait to settle their differences permanently...and for all the states and the peoples of the region to settle the conflicts that divide the Arabs from Israel." In the following months, Baker alone made eight trips to the Middle East in an effort to renew the peace process.

This whole period was a very special time in history. Communism was nearing collapse in the Soviet Union (the United States and the Russians had even cooperated during the Gulf War crisis), and the United States was emerging as the undisputed and sole superpower in the world. No less unusual was the cooperation that had emerged in the Middle East, epitomized by the fact that Syria, Egypt, and Saudi Arabia had worked in tandem with the United States against a fellow Arab nation. Washington believed that this new level of cooperation could be mustered, at the very least, into a drive that could establish Palestinian-Israeli peace talks—talks that, once and for all, might actually succeed.

It seems to me that the Iraq war impacted Israeli thinking in a way that made many Israelis more open than in the past to making territorial compromises. The Gulf War had demonstrated that for all of Israel's military might, it was unable on its own to defend itself against attacking SCUD missiles. Sure, without American military support, Israel would have retaliated against Iraqi attacks, but it couldn't stop the missiles on its own. Therefore, an increasing number of Israelis were open to the idea that the only surefire method to protect Israel and its citizens was through a comprehensive peace agreement with the Arab world. And the sooner the better. Saddam's missiles had not been armed with biological and chemical warheads, as Israel had feared, but the threat of some future hostile Arab leader sending forth such missiles was increasingly real. And then, it would not only be Israeli soldiers at risk, but the entire society, with a potential for unimaginably high casualties. Just a few years earlier, President Reagan's secretary of state, George Shultz, had argued that missiles would change future warfare in the region, and most people simply ignored his words. But now, Shultz's thesis had been proven. In just a few days in January, Saddam Hussein had made it clear that the pushing of a button could put far more Israeli lives at risk than the dispatching of battalions of Arab troops.

In June 1991, six months after the beginning of the Gulf War, President Bush sent letters to the Arab leaders and to Prime Minister Shamir, outlining his desire to hold a peace conference in the autumn. Weeks passed, but Syrian President Assad did not bother to reply, and it was obvious that his refusal to do so was hindering other Arab leaders from responding as well.

Baker, in an unusual turn of phrase, announced that he was prepared to "leave the dead cat at the door" of the nation that stood in the way of the conference; in other words, he was perfectly willing to publicly point fingers at those nations who declined the invitation to attend the conference and thereby put obstacles in the way of peace. In diplomatic terms, Baker's statement was regarded as a hefty threat.

Everybody knew where Mubarak stood. He and the

Egyptian leadership had been pushing for negotiations ever since the Camp David accords. And Jordan's King Hussein had, over the years, engaged in secret negotiations with Israeli leaders. But Assad had long been regarded as the most intractable—and the most cunning—of the Arab leaders. If he would agree to attend the conference, all the other Arab leaders would fall in line. And once that would happen, Israel, with its own rather uncompromising prime minister, Yitzhak Shamir, would have no choice but to participate as well.

In fact, I remember thinking that Shamir was banking on Syrian refusal, which would spare him from being blamed for the conference's failure.

Wayne and I were engaged at the time in our own acts of private diplomacy to help bring the conference about. We met with Prime Minister Shamir on July 5. He was not particularly friendly; his manner was, in fact, brusque. But he did have a message for us to bring to President Assad (Wayne's connections as a congressman had enabled him to schedule a meeting for us). We were to tell Assad that what Israel wanted was "negotiations without long statements and obstacles, without fanfare, celebrations and spotlights." In other words, if Assad was serious about negotiating with Israel, he should meet with Israel one-on-one, either through secret channels or openly, instead of sending a delegation, as one of many Arab delegations, to a public conference. It was clear both from our meeting with Shamir and from the statements we heard attributed to him, that he regarded this conference as a ruse to put unfair pressure on Israel and to make Israel look bad.

Assad, we already knew, was hesitant to start negotiating with Israel because he was unclear as to what Israel would be willing to offer. Thus, if it turned out that Israel had no intention of returning the entire Golan Heights— and anything less than that would be unacceptable to Assad—then there would be no point for him to meet with any representatives from Israel. All that would happen is that Israel would gain diplomatic leverage by seeming to be a nation seeking peace, while Syria would look like the bad guys.

It was clear to me from our first meeting with Assad that he had very definite ideas about the sort of relationship he envisaged with Israel. He was willing to accept Israel as a reality. But he saw no need to reward Israel with a peace treaty even if it returned the Golan, and certainly not if it didn't. As he explained to us and, as I am sure, he explained to many dozens, if not hundreds, of others, the Golan was Syria's territory and it had been stolen from Syria by Israel. The truth is, he spoke of the Golan in even more personal terms, as territory that had been stolen from him by the Israelis. Why therefore should he have to enter into negotiations to get back what had been stolen from him? I remember the analogy he used: "If someone comes into your house and steals a picture, are you going to give him something to bring your picture back? Why should you do that? The man who stole it is a criminal. He should return the picture and he should go to jail. I mean, you should certainly not give the man a reward for returning what is yours."

What occurred to me when I had spoken to Assad was not only that he was forgetting the provocative behavior of Syria in 1967 that had prompted Israel to take over the Golan Heights, but that he also was turning UN Resolutions 242 and 338—the resolutions that essentially supported the idea of exchanging land for peace—on their head. His interpretation of 242 seemed to be, "First, Israel must return the land it acquired in war illegally, then maybe Syria will consider peaceful relations."

Assad also made it clear to us that he was uncomfortable conducting negotiations under the auspices of the superpowers, the United States and the Soviet Union (at the time, the Soviet Union was still regarded as a superpower). He preferred to see the negotiations mediated by the UN. According to Edward Djerejian, the American ambassador to Syria, what Assad craved was "the legal umbrella of the United Nations." After all, he was hinging his case on United Nations Security Council Resolutions 242 and 338, and he assumed he could achieve the best results, therefore, meeting under UN auspices. Also, as Assad and everyone else in the world knew, the UN was overwhelmingly unsympathetic to Israel.

At our July meeting with Shamir, he had anticipated these arguments of Assad's, most notably for his demand that Israel announce in advance its intention to return the Golan. If Assad raised this argument, he advised us to tell him: "In negotiations, if you ask for the end, there will never be a beginning. Let's start negotiations without preconditions. You cannot know the results of negotiations in the beginning. And even if we get partial results, that, too, is good." Unfortunately, I knew that last line, "even if we get partial results, that, too, is good," would not strike Assad as good.

In addition to Wayne and myself, we brought Stephen P. Cohen, a professor of conflict resolution at Harvard, along to Syria. Ambassador Djerejian came as well. The Syrians sent an old helicopter to take us to the meeting at Assad's vacation home in Latakia, a port city on the Mediterranean. The sounds inside the ancient Soviet chopper were deafening and the vibrations so powerful that it seemed that the copter might self-destruct. When we arrived in Latakia, we headed straight to Assad's retreat. It was a particularly beautiful day, and I remember his villa well. It was located on a cliff that looked at the distant mountains on one side, and the brilliant Mediterranean beaches on the other.

Ambassador Djerejian told us that he had had a definite strategy in mind in pushing to arrange this meeting with the president. He thought it was important that Assad be exposed to a wide range of opinions, which meant that he should not only meet with government officials, congressmen, and senators, but with American citizens from different walks of life. He figured that the discussions that could occur with private citizens like me might be more frank and even more helpful in finding ways to break through the psychological barriers.

Over the years, Assad and I developed what I can only regard as a warm relationship. We had a grasp of each other's reality. I knew what he could do, and I knew what he couldn't do.

I know that Assad did many ruthless things, and of course, if I wanted our attempts at achieving peace to fail, I could always choose to activate those feelings of anger over the bad things he had done. I knew that he was capable of personally dispensing people from this world without a second thought, as he had done in Hama.*

But I also know enough history to know that all leaders make tough and cruel decisions that sometimes lead to

---

* In the early 1980s a revolt against Assad was started in Hama, the fifth-largest city in Syria. Assad surrounded the town with tanks, shelled it, and then rolled the tanks into the town's center. It is estimated that over 20,000 people were killed in the putting down of this revolt.

the deaths of many people, most of them innocent. Assad rationalized the killings he committed by arguing that his enemies were therefore the sworn enemies of Syria.

My decision, therefore, even at that first meeting, was to constantly remind myself that I was there for a purpose. And that purpose was the greater good, the saving of many lives; therefore, my friendship with Assad was not a sanctioning of his past actions, but was rather guided by my desire to make the future better and more peaceful, and without killing. That was my job as I understood it. So that if I could achieve better results and save lives by creating an atmosphere of friendship with Assad, that's what I was going to do.

When I first met Assad, he was considerably taller than I expected, and his face looked elongated. I knew that he had been a pilot in his youth, so I expected him to be somewhat rugged-looking and in good physical condition. Being a bit of a physical fitness devotee myself, I was, therefore, struck by the fact that he looked somewhat frail. He certainly didn't look like a man who exercised much. On the other hand, once we started to talk, I was impressed by how bright he was; he was clearly attuned to the nuances of everything that was said. He also was charming, and funny—which I certainly had not expected—and an interesting raconteur when talking about his past.

That meeting, and most of the subsequent meetings we had with him, lasted three to four hours, and most of the talking was done by him.

We met in the large reception area of his home. After greetings and ceremonial pictures, Wayne told Assad that the noisy helicopter he had sent for us had blocked up his ears, and suggested that Assad buy some American helicopters instead. Assad laughed: "We cannot enter this area. It would violate the taboo [against American arms sales to Syria]."

When we sat down, I noticed the rigid manner in which he spoke, barely gesturing with his long slim hands. He also carefully monitored the reactions of his guests to what he was saying, and when someone addressed him, he would look the person straight in the eye the whole time he was speaking.

Wayne, acutely conscious of his role there as an American congressman, jumped quickly to the main point of our visit: "The whole world," he told Assad, "is waiting and watching for Syria's response to the letter from our president." Wayne informed him that he himself was personally committed to Secretary of State Baker's policies 100 percent. He also told Assad—I suppose he was trying to be both lighthearted and a little heavy-handed at the same time—that Ambassador Djerejian was set to be promoted to assistant secretary of state for the Middle East, but that the president had told him, "Don't come home until you bring the answer to my letter." Wayne went on for a few minutes longer and finally concluded his pitch on a surprisingly direct and undiplomatic note: "So, Mr. President, we have come for the letter."

Assad, to none of our surprise, was evasive and unwilling to be pressured. "We will shortly answer President Bush's letter. President Bush's letter has been studied with the care it deserves."

Figuring that there was little to be gained by further pursuing that issue, I relayed to him what Prime Minister Shamir had told us about his desire to initiate substantial negotiations with Syria. Again, in an effort to lighten the atmosphere, I added: "I invited him to come with us, but Shamir said, 'I don't think they'd give me a visa.'"

"Perhaps this is one of the few statements from Mr. Shamir that was ever right," Assad joked. But he immediately turned serious and made it clear that he would not meet with Israel, as Shamir wanted, without preconditions. "Mr. Shamir asks, 'Why preconditions?'" Because Syria, Assad emphasized, intended to negotiate with Israel on the basis of the UN resolutions, which meant "land for peace." Shamir obviously did not intend to abide by this condition, and to return all the land Israel had taken from Syria. "My belief," Assad said, is "that [therefore] he is not serious." And with that ended our efforts at that meeting to convey Shamir's appeal to Assad for direct Israeli-Syrian negotiations.

Indeed, Assad now returned to the subject of the international peace conference, and insisted that all the clarifications he was sure Israel would insist on before attending the conference would torpedo it, and end up making it ineffective.

Wayne took Assad's comment as an opening to make another appeal. "You're the master of putting the ball in the other person's court," he began. And given that King Hussein was ready to go forward, and that Mubarak was ready to come to Madrid as well, but only with Syria's cooperation, then if Syria consented to come, Israel would be pressed to do so as well, and to negotiate seriously. In addition, because of Syria's recent participation in the Desert Storm alliance, the Syrian-American relationship had improved substantially. Wayne did caution Assad though to be realistic about what he could expect from the United States. "Congress is very supportive and involved with Israel. We will not impose our ideas on Israel. We support a strong secure Israel."

Assad was actually less offended by Wayne's last words than I thought he would be and, in a curious way, I found his response somewhat reassuring: "For the U.S. to support the security of Israel is no problem, but not to support Israeli aggression."

Assad now introduced yet another element. He was opposed to any nation making a separate peace with Israel, as Egypt had done twelve years earlier. "We want a real, just, and comprehensive solution. We are against any separate agreement. It will only lead to more war."

In other words, I understood him to be saying, Israel would not be able to negotiate an agreement with Syria, as it had done with Egypt, without resolving once and for all the Palestinian issue.

At the end of the meeting, Assad made a very short statement, but I found in it a hint that he would agree to come to the conference: "We will continue to respond to the U.S. efforts to reach peace." I remember thinking that it sounded like he was telegraphing his moves before he actually made them. In a way, this would make things seem more low-key and cause less turmoil and excitement when he announced his decision to come. And indeed, six days after the meeting, he sent a letter to Ambassador Djerejian formally announcing that Syria would attend the peace conference.

With Syria's acceptance in hand, it was clear that the international conference would happen; there could now be no substantial Arab opposition to the gathering. And with the Arab nations all willing to support it, Israel would not be in a position to say no.

Baker saw Assad's acceptance as very important, and a crucial bargaining chip in America's negotiations with Israel. As he noted in his memoirs, he could now go to Prime Minister Shamir and tell him that a new age had dawned. The Arab states were willing to engage in direct negotiations with Israel, something they had steadfastly refused to do, and something that had been Israel's stated goal for over forty years. "I calculated that neither Shamir nor the Palestinians could possibly remain intransigent in these circumstances."

On October 30, the Madrid peace conference opened. The two chairs were Presidents Bush and Gorbachev. Most of the speeches that first day were filled with accusations and with fury, hardly the sort of talks designed to bring about an atmosphere of peace and of reconciliation. Thus, Prime Minister Shamir railed against Syria, depicting it as a terrorist state. Syria's foreign minister, Faruk Al-Shara, responded by displaying a half-century-old wanted poster of Shamir distributed by the British in the 1940s, at a time when Shamir was one of the three leaders of Lehi (Freedom Fighters of Israel), an anti-British terror organization that had, among other actions, assassinated Lord Walter Edward Guinness Moyne—the British minister of state for the Middle East—in Egypt in 1944. Israel might accuse Syria of supporting terrorism, Al-Shara seemed to be saying, but what an odd accusation to be made by a man who had spent his early adult years running a terrorist organization.

Amid the bitter denunciations being leveled that morning, the one great positive was that the delegates, representing Israel, Egypt, Syria, Lebanon, and a joint Jordan-Palestinian delegation, were actually sitting down together around a large T-shaped table.*

Yet another potentially encouraging step was that Prime Minister Shamir had chosen to personally head the

---

* Other participants included the United States, Russia, the European Community, the Gulf Cooperation Council, which sent its secretary general to the conference as an observer, and the United Nations, which sent an observer, representing the secretary-general.

Israeli delegation, instead of sending his foreign minister, as Syria, for example, had done. Why Shamir chose to come is still not fully clear. Some speculated that he wanted to be the one announcing that Israel would walk out of the conference if the Palestinian delegation consisted of PLO members; in consequence—and to forestall the conference from coming to a quick end—none of the Palestinian delegates had a direct affiliation with the PLO. But all this was nothing more than a pretense. It was an open secret, known to Shamir and to everyone in attendance, that the Palestinian delegates were in constant touch with the PLO leadership; the word was that the PLO heads were ensconced in a nearby hotel, from which they were dispatching messages as to what the Palestinian delegates should say.

I can only conjecture that Shamir had an additional, more positive, reason to come to Madrid: to try and cultivate a better relationship both with President Bush and President Gorbachev. Because of his reputation for being stubborn and uncompromising, Shamir may well have thought he would get "p.r. points" merely for showing up and thereby shore up his rather fragile relationship with President Bush, as well as demonstrate to the Israeli public that he was serious about peace.

Also, attendance in Madrid involved little domestic risk for Shamir. Ninety-one percent of Israelis favored the talks, though only 37 percent thought any good would come from them. In the well-chosen words of a columnist for *Ha'aretz*—Israel's most respected newspaper—the country was divided between "skeptics and pessimists."

Within days the Conference had ended, and Israel now found herself starting direct talks with Jordan, Syria, and Lebanon. As regards the Palestinians, the main problem in getting the talks going was reaching an agreement on venue. Israel wanted the talks held in Israel, but Palestinian negotiator Hanan Ashrawi was adamantly opposed: "We cannot negotiate under duress," she protested, "subject to curfew, censorship, imprisonment, and deportation. We need a neutral place in which we can move freely and our security is guaranteed."

Ashrawi's concerns struck me as somewhat exaggerated. Shamir might not have been the most tolerant of men, particularly in his attitude toward the Palestinian leadership, but the likelihood that he would have summoned them to Israel and then subjected them to "curfew, censorship, imprisonment, and deportation," struck me as pretty remote.

From the vantage point of 2005, fourteen years since Madrid, was anything achieved there? I do believe that some important and positive precedents were established. I think one could plausibly make the case that the discussions initiated in Madrid became the foundation for the Jordanian-Israeli peace treaty of 1994, and might even have formed the basis for the subsequent series of interim agreements with the Palestinians.

It also is likely that the Conference affected attitudes in Israel more than had been anticipated, opening up among Israelis a greater optimism about the possibility of speaking to their neighbors. In any case, within months of Madrid, Prime Minister Shamir's government collapsed. The Labor Party came to power under the leadership of Yitzhak Rabin. There was no question that Rabin would be more open than Shamir to reaching a settlement with the Palestinians, and with all of Israel's neighbors, for that matter. Indeed, because of Rabin's much greater openness to making territorial compromises, there was much more incentive for the

Palestinians and for Syria to be open to negotiations with Israel. Indeed, there are those who argue that the Madrid Conference essentially started Israel on an inevitable path of separation from the territories.

Rabin's election made me more optimistic on the peace front for yet another reason. He had impeccable military credentials—Rabin was a former Army chief of staff, a hero of the Six-Day War, and the defense minister in Shamir's government—and therefore, it seemed to me that he would have the luxury of being flexible on territorial issues without causing Israelis to panic on issues of security. Whoever knew Rabin, and he had been a public figure for so long that most Israelis knew and trusted him, was confident that he would never compromise on issues of defense even for the elusive dream of peace. In other words, if Rabin told Israelis that a certain area of land could be given back without causing risk, they would believe him. On the other hand, had someone with a more left-wing agenda—or someone with a lesser background in army and security matters—told them such a thing, they would not.

Secretary of State Baker soon came calling on the new prime minister, and Rabin responded by canceling 6,000 housing units that were scheduled to be constructed in the West Bank. Then, when President Bush announced that the United States would stand behind $10 billion worth of loan guarantees to Israel—an announcement he was unwilling to make when Shamir was in power—Wayne and I found it a lot easier to start imagining a more optimistic future.

Meanwhile, changes were coming to the U.S. political landscape as well. Although the president had achieved a 70 percent approval rating after the 1991 Gulf War, the more recent economic malaise had caused his approval

rating to plummet—as he approached the 1992 election—to 30 percent. This in turn caused him to recruit
Baker as his campaign manager, thereby effectively ending Baker's active involvement in Mideast diplomacy.
Foreign affairs matters now shifted to Lawrence Eagle-
burger and Ed Djerejian (who had indeed received his
State Department promotion after procuring President
Assad's agreement to come to Madrid), and it was clear to
everyone that, for President Bush, matters of foreign affairs had fallen by the wayside.

Even so, it seemed apparent in the summer of 1992
that the winds of change were affecting the region. Israeli
officials, for example, used the word "withdrawal" in negotiations and, even more remarkable, Syrian President
Assad spoke—in front of cameras no less—about a
"peace of the brave,"* a phrase that was understood as
meaning that Syria might actually be willing to establish
peaceful relations with Israel—as opposed to a mere non-
belligerency pact—in exchange for the return of the
Golan Heights.

Harry Truman famously said that his most ardent
wish was for a one-handed economist since every economist who ever advised him always finished his
presentation by saying, "On the other hand." Similarly,
with all the indications of potential improvements in relations both between Israel and the Palestinians and
between Israel and Syria, on the other hand, something
very worrisome was going on as well. Hamas, a new
force, was gaining ground in the Arab world, and it was
spreading through the Palestinian and broader Arab
world like wildfire. It seemed that Hamas and its brand

---

* This was a phrase Arafat later started to use, and which, I believe, was first coined by French president Charles de Gaulle.

of Islamism had come in part as the replacement for the old-style Arab nationalism. But whereas Arab nationalism in the past had generally been secular in orientation, Islamism was rooting Arab unity in religion, combining the extreme elements of nationalism and Islamic fundamentalism.

Ironically, during the PLO's earlier, more rejectionist days, the Israeli leadership had actually regarded the rise of Hamas as a positive development. They understood the organization's goal as restricted to bringing about a revived commitment to Islam among the largely irreligious Palestinian population, and therefore saw it as an alternative—and likely a less dangerous alternative—to the PLO. Unfortunately, what was now becoming apparent was that the religion preached by Hamas was not one of love, at least not toward non-Muslims and Muslims who did not accept its teachings. The organization's theology was an angry one, and wherever Hamas established a foothold, violence followed. Evidence of that was apparent in Gaza and the West Bank. In those Palestinian universities where Hamas thrived, zealous activists poured acid on the faces of female students who did not wear the hejab (the traditional Muslim head scarf), and who refused to dress in the clothing the extremists regarded as modest.

Those Israelis who had hoped that Hamas would emerge as an alternative to the PLO were right. But, boy, did they come to rue this alternative. Hamas—today associated in people's minds with "suicide bombers"— very quickly became far more radical and ruthless than the PLO. Indeed, just as the PLO was shifting to a more nuanced and pragmatic position toward Israel—most notably advocating a two-state solution and the right of

Israel to exist as a Jewish state—Hamas was growing ever more extreme in its rejection of Israel and of the West. In Hamas's eyes, Israel was a criminal outpost of decadent western values, and had been imported into the Middle East to destroy the Muslim world. Not only had Israel stolen the land of the Palestinians, its loathsome values were wreaking destruction on Muslim values as well.

Accompanied by its willingness to provide food and social services to its largely poor constituency, Hamas found that its message—destroy Israel, Israelis, and Israeli soldiers, by any means possible—was resonating among tens of thousands of Palestinians and others throughout the Arab world. Already by 1991, some 25 percent of Palestinians were identifying with Hamas. This meant that even when Israel killed Hamas leaders and terrorist operatives, there were dozens, maybe hundreds, more Palestinians offering themselves to replace the fallen fighters.

Throughout the latter part of 1992, more and more Israeli soldiers were being killed. It was rarely very large numbers at a time—three soldiers shot and killed in a jeep in Gaza, another killed and two more wounded in a similar ambush in Hebron—but the numbers were accumulating, and Israelis were growing disheartened and angrier.

December 15, 1992, was the day that Prime Minister Rabin finally lost his cool. On that day, the body of an Israeli border policeman who had been kidnapped by Hamas agents was identified by pathologists. The patrolman's hands had been tied behind his back, and he had then been knifed.

Rabin concluded that the time had come to send a clear message to the Palestinians, PLO and Hamas alike.

Negotiations might be going on with Palestinian representatives in Washington, but a policy of negotiation should not be confused with a policy of weakness. And so, Rabin pushed through his cabinet a decision to expel some 415 Palestinian leaders and supporters of terrorism onto the Lebanese border. Rabin and the cabinet understood that this decision would be controversial; Israel had certainly never taken an action of so broad a scope before.

I remember this period very well. Two days before the patrolman's body was found, Wayne and I met with Arafat. We had been picked up in Tunis by Sami Mussalam, Arafat's chief of staff, and taken to one of Arafat's many safehouses.

The Palestinians were in a very upbeat mood. Rumors were circulating that Israel would soon repeal the legal bans on dealing with the PLO. This meant that the two sides might soon be talking directly. Abu Mazen, who, years later, would become the Palestinians' prime minister and later president, told us: "We are eager to start a new phase of life in the Middle East."

What had inspired much of this optimism was Rabin's public pronouncements distinguishing between the issue of security and the issue of settlements. In other words, as Abu Mazen understood his remarks, Rabin was making it clear that Israel was open to making decisions on the basis of security needs alone, and not on the basis of political and ideological considerations. If Rabin did not feel ideologically constrained to expand or even keep most of the settlements, there would be much greater room for territorial compromise.

That day, as we spoke, we were envisaging the type of measures that could raise the quality of life of the Palestinians, and that would result—to Israel's benefit—in a decline in terrorism. Terrorism, as the PLO representatives argued, was fueled by three things in particular: constant friction with Israeli troops; the omnipresent barbed wire fences; and a stagnant economy. But if Israel started cooperating in economic ventures with the Palestinians, the Palestinians, in turn, would have reason to turn to groups other than the terrorists. It was not a subject the PLO had broached before. Indeed, as Abu Mazen confided that day: "We are willing to cooperate economically, which we have never been willing to do before." Arafat, as well, kept emphasizing how economic cooperation would create common Israeli-Palestinian interests, and these interests—more than armies and weapons—would motivate and enable the two sides to resolve their disputes.

Wayne had often emphasized how economic interaction could drive the peace process. Since Israeli and Palestinians alike would have to give up some national dreams—the Israelis would have to part with the overwhelming majority of the West Bank, and the Palestinians would have to relinquish their dream of conquering Israel—it was particularly important that each side feel they were gaining something tangible from coming to an agreement. And while a peaceful resolution of the conflict would result in fewer deaths (fewer Palestinians would be killed in battles with Israeli soldiers, and fewer Israelis would die through terrorist attacks), this alone would not satisfy the Palestinians, many of whom were living in such dire poverty that life did not necessarily seem preferable to death in battle. But if the quality of life started to rise in the West Bank and Gaza, and there was hope that it would continue to rise, then the Palestinian people would have a tangible reason to prefer peace to war. People become conservative, it has been said, when they have something worth conserving. The Palestinians might become less drawn to radicalism when a peaceful, economically viable approach would yield them some benefits.

Arafat, Abu Mazen, Abu Ala, Saeb Erekat, and the others present kept emphasizing to me that what they needed from Israel was concrete, helpful steps. Thus, Israel was angry because of the soldiers that were being killed but, as Israel well knew, far more Palestinians were dying than Jews, and these deaths were fueling Palestinian rage. How much longer could Arafat try and sell the Palestinians on the advantages to be gained by negotiating with Israel? The negotiations had to bear fruit, but the Israelis were being ungenerous and intransigent. ("Israeli intransigence" had long been a favorite subject of almost every Arab leader with whom I was in contact.)

Aside from the focus on economic initiatives, the conversation did not seem to be going anywhere new, until Arafat suddenly surprised us with some potentially good news: "I will tell you something very confidentially which I have not mentioned to anyone else. Three days ago, a man came from Hebron to say that Rabin wanted to start a back channel consultation with us."

It was hard to understand exactly what he meant. A man came from Hebron. The words sounded almost biblical. But who was it who came? Arafat didn't elaborate, but the news, if accurate, was major. Talks had been going on for weeks between the Israelis and the Palestinians in Washington, but had been going nowhere. One reason of course was that because of the publicity surrounding them, neither Palestinian nor Israeli representatives were willing to make any dramatic proposals. It is hard to put forward breakthrough proposals when you know that what you say will be reported, and will subject you to vituperous attacks from members of your own community who will accuse you at best of selling out and, at worst, of being a traitor.

In any case, the talks were floundering so badly that, at one point, Avi Gil, Shimon Peres's chief of staff, had sent the foreign ministry a transcript of the discussions, with the dates whited out. No one at the foreign ministry could put the documents in order because the talks had just circled round and round, with no headway.

But there was another, far more fundamental, reason the talks were not making any headway. The Palestinian delegates had been vetted by the Israelis to ensure they were not PLO members. But, in practical terms, all that this meant was the Palestinian representatives in Washington wouldn't make a move without clearing it with the PLO leadership. Therefore, whenever the Israelis raised an issue to which the response wasn't obvious, the Palestinian representatives would not respond until they faxed Arafat and received an answer.

By establishing a secret channel, the unnecessary and time-wasting middlemen would be removed. And, by having the discussions carried out in secret—without constant leaks to the press—the peace process could be greatly accelerated.

Arafat told us that his first response to Rabin's proposal was no, not because he opposed back-door communications in principle, but because Rabin had wanted the talks to take place in Europe, "and I want it to go on in Cairo so that it can be kept confidential—which it can't be in Europe."

Then Arafat expressed one additional concern, and it now became apparent that this was the reason he had been so anxious to meet with us. He needed to know: "Was the proposal to establish a secret channel between Rabin and Arafat a real one? Did it come from Rabin? I would like for you to verify this."

Wayne and I were obviously excited. Here we were, two private citizens (Wayne, by this point, was an ex-congressman) whose mission in life was to bolster Israeli-Palestinian peace efforts, and what Arafat was now banking on was that we had high-level contacts across the Arab, Israeli, and American worlds alike, contacts that few others had. But what he did not know was that, while our relationship with Foreign Minister Peres—and with the right-wing Ariel Sharon, for that matter—was very close, our relationship with Rabin, the very man Arafat wanted us to meet, was more impersonal.

The very advantages that Wayne and I had in meeting with people like Arafat and Peres—that we were private citizens and beholden to no one—were the very traits, I believe, that somewhat alienated Rabin from us. Rather than seeing us as useful conduits, I had the feeling that he saw us as meddlesome, naïve do-gooders. At our first meeting with Rabin after he became prime minister, Wayne asked him, "Mr. Prime Minister, can we do anything to help you?"

Rabin, renowned for many virtues of which tact was not the most prominent, responded with one word, "No." In describing this incident to a friend, Wayne later remarked: "There was a fifteen-second sigh while I picked myself up off the floor."

Nonetheless, we told Arafat we would be sure to relay his question directly to Rabin.

We arrived in Israel three days later. It was too late in

the evening to schedule any meetings, and it was not until the following morning that we learned about the Israeli decision to deport the 415 Palestinians. It didn't take a prophet to realize the fireworks this expulsion would set off throughout the Arab world (and the wider world as well), and throughout the Palestinian world, in particular. The already hard job of those interested in furthering the peace process was, we understood, about to get much harder.

By now, more reports about the deportation were emerging, and they were having an even worse effect than we would have predicted. Many of the suspects aboard the buses were drawn from the approximately 300 Palestinian activists who had been arrested since September. And in the days since the soldier had been kidnapped, the Israeli army had arrested an additional 1,300 Hamas and Islamic Jihad activists. Once Rabin made the decision to carry out the deportations, he instructed the Mossad, army intelligence, and the army's legal advocate to comb through the 1,600 detainees and handpick 400 or so terrorist leaders. With only several hours to leaf through so many dossiers, errors were made, a fact that the legal advocate, to his credit, quickly recognized and acknowledged.

By this time, the buses, with the prisoners blindfolded and handcuffed, had already left, and were streaming toward the Lebanese border. Although the government had hoped to keep word of the deportations secret, the news had leaked out even as the buses were en route. Israeli civil libertarians immediately procured a Supreme Court injunction to freeze the order of deportation while the court explored its legality. Because of the injunction, the buses were halted in Metulla, on Israel's far northern border. There, thirty-five prisoners who had wrongfully been arrested were removed from the buses and were replaced by thirty-two other prisoners who had been flown northward.

Strangely enough, it was army chief of staff Ehud Barak—a man who years later came to be regarded as perhaps the most dovish prime minister in Israel's history—who had first proposed the idea of banishing Palestinian troublemakers, and it was Justice Minister Dan Meridor, a man of the right, who had shot it down. (Meridor regarded it as illegal, and also recognized what a scandal it would cause.) Over a period of several months, Barak had repeatedly tried to get this measure considered, only to have it squelched each time. But then he raised it with the prime minister once more, right after the border patrolman's body was found. And this time, Rabin was receptive and pushed the proposal through the Cabinet, eliciting the support even of Cabinet members who had previously rejected the idea of deportation. How did Rabin convince them?

Rabin argued that a blow to Hamas would help Palestinian moderates and accelerate the peace process. Hamas, as everyone knew, was growing increasingly popular within the West Bank and Gaza, and their unmitigated hatred of Israel posed a serious threat to future negotiations. Israeli intelligence recently learned that they were planning the assassination of more moderate Palestinian figures, such as Faisel Husseini, the chief Palestinian negotiator with Israel; there were also reports that Hamas was planning terrorist attacks directed at Israeli schools.

Furthermore, Rabin argued, banishment for up to two years was legal both under Israeli and international law, and was less damaging than destroying homes, shutting down mosques, or even introducing the death penalty.

And just in case these arguments were insufficient to bring some of the more left-wing members of his Cabinet into line, Rabin added that he had talked with the far right Tsomet Party about joining the government. The implication seemed obvious: if the Cabinet rejected the expulsions, Rabin might drop the left-wing Meretz Party from his coalition, and replace them with rightists.

In the end, the entire Cabinet, with one abstention, voted to approve the expulsions. Shulamit Aloni, one of the most left-wing members of the Cabinet, argued that doing so was necessary to preserve what she called the "peace government."

In the drama of the moment, not one Cabinet member asked Rabin just how many Hamas leaders he was planning to expel.

The Israeli Supreme Court quickly ruled that the expulsion was legal. The Hamas members were then bussed across the Israeli-controlled security zone in southern Lebanon and released in a six-mile-wide no-man's-land between Israeli and Lebanese troops. The men were given blankets, some food, and fifty dollars each. But when they approached the nearest Lebanese army post, the Lebanese troops, backed by armored vehicles and tanks, stopped them from entering Lebanese territory. Lebanon had no intention of helping Israel rid itself of people Israel regarded as enemies. Nor, I would guess, did the Lebanese government see any gain for itself in increasing its Hamas population by over 400, most of whom were leaders.

Israel had not counted on Lebanon's reaction and, when the exiles started heading back in the direction of Israel, Israeli soldiers fired bullets over their heads.

The men hunkered down in a rocky patch a mile or so from a Lebanese army post (the Lebanese might not welcome them, but weren't shooting in their direction, either), and vowed to stay there in protest. It was the dead of winter in southern Lebanon, and temperatures hovered around 20 degrees. News media soon showed up to film the suffering men. In the lens of the camera, one did not see firebrand extremists arguing for Israel's destruction; instead, one saw cold, miserable victims of the Israeli government, men who did not look dangerous at all. The public relations disaster intensified as, for three weeks, neither the Israelis nor the Lebanese permitted the Red Cross to pass through either of their borders to supply aid to the fundamentalists. Finally, Israel relented, and allowed the Red Cross through.

Needless to say, the whole event was turning into an increasing fiasco and black eye for Israel. To boot, the PLO, who were in fact no great friends of Hamas, announced that Palestinian participation in the peace talks would be suspended until the expelled men were returned home. So much for Rabin's insistence that this blow to Hamas would help Palestinian moderates and accelerate the peace process.

What Rabin's order of expulsion did reveal was his limited understanding of Palestinian politics and sensibilities. How could he imagine that the more moderate forces within the Palestinian community would ignore what Rabin had done to the Hamas detainees and continue dealing with the Israelis on a "business as usual" basis? Even if in their hearts, the other Palestinian leaders were pleased to see a harsh blow dealt to Hamas, they certainly could not publicly act as if they were pleased. Their constituents, whose goodwill mattered far more to them than Rabin's, would regard them as traitors for acquiescing in an order of expulsion issued against fellow Palestinians. For over forty years, the Palestinians had been arguing that Israel had expelled hundreds of thousands of Palestinians during the 1948 War. The symbolism of Israel once again expelling Palestinians was too awful for more moderate Palestinian leaders to ignore. Faisel Husseini—the man whose life Rabin claimed to be safeguarding by going after Hamas—cancelled talks with Israel for months, as the Palestinians mourned over, and insisted on the return of, the deported men.

Worse—from Rabin and Israel's perspective—because the deportees were seen by the Palestinian populace as martyrs for the Palestinian cause, their expulsion caused Hamas to grow in legitimacy. And Rabin, who later proved to be so forthcoming in his openness to the Palestinians, was now being perceived as a hardheaded, short-sighted, loose cannon. He had rammed through this order of expulsion policy behind the backs of his foreign minister, Shimon Peres, who was in Asia at the time, and Danny Rothschild, the army's chief administrator over the territories. And, of course, the one achievement that might have justified the policy never happened: The Hamas attacks continued.

Ha'aretz commentator Doron Rosenbloom compared Rabin's expulsion order to Shamir's collision with President Bush over settlements: "Suddenly we had another Captain Ahab completely enamored of some colossal mistake that carried with it a great principle, a mighty idea for which he was prepared to endanger everything."

It was into this siege mentality—with a highly defensive Rabin lashing out at his critics—that Wayne and I arrived in Israel with our question from Arafat: Was the offer of a backdoor for real?

Both Wayne and I believed that much as Rabin disliked Arafat and wanted nothing to do with him, he was the only game in town. If Rabin wanted to find a solution to Israel's conflict with the Palestinians, with whom else could he reach an agreement?

We tried to get through to the prime minister in several different ways. On December 18, we met with Major General Uri Saguy, the director of military intelligence. What I remember most about that meeting was how much Saguy seemed to agree with us. His words paralleled Wayne's and my thinking: "With whom do we negotiate? Who is left? Who has remained?—only Arafat."

That same morning, Dr. Stephen P. Cohen, who worked with us, met with Eitan Haber, Rabin's chief of staff, and informed him of Arafat's request from us.

But Rabin did not get back to us, and seemed to have no interest in dealing with us. Quite possibly, he had no desire to rely on a team of civilians on a matter of such delicacy. Also, he might have felt that the fewer people who knew about potentially secret negotiations, the greater their chance of secrecy. And the less chance that they would fail.

But whatever Rabin's reasons for declining to meet with us, we would have to return to Tunis empty-handed.

Wayne, bitter at Rabin's acting as a Lone Ranger—leaving his own foreign minister out of the process—remarked on how much he wished that Peres was prime minister, just as he wished that he had been elected a senator two years earlier, but that, "in both cases, we had to adjust to the realities."

We boarded the plane to Tunis with a sense of regret. I didn't look forward to telling Arafat that we had been totally unsuccessful at getting a response from the prime minister to his question. All we would be able to offer Arafat was our assessment of the current conditions in Israel, and that did not strike me as enough to justify our meeting with him in Tunis.

At the airport, we were met by Sami Mussalam, Arafat's chief of staff, along with a cadre of security guards. Mussalam appeared visibly downcast throughout the drive to the house where Arafat was staying.

"Maybe we shouldn't have come," I said to him.

It hardly improved my mood when he sighed in response, "Maybe."

Despite our expectations, Arafat received us very warmly. At dinner, he personally served Wayne and me, placing pieces of meat on Wayne's plate, and vegetables on mine. When the actual discussion began, at about one in the morning, Arafat surprised us by not acting at all discouraged. Instead, he seemed as enthusiastic as ever about the peace process.

He did however have his own take on the expulsions and on Rabin's motivations and, needless to say, it was totally at variance with what Rabin had argued before his Cabinet. According to Arafat, Rabin could not possibly have believed that what he would do would weaken Hamas: "It was no accident. He knew that security measures against one group does not weaken them." In Arafat's view, Rabin's behavior had been intended to damage the PLO by strengthening Hamas, who would now be seen as the more ardent fighters against Israel.

To my mind, Arafat's analysis displayed a grave misunderstanding of Rabin's intentions. It was clear to all who knew Rabin that he believed that harsh measures against Hamas leaders would scare the group into submission. And the truth is, for all the Palestinian and international outcries, Rabin and his experts still believed Hamas had been badly, perhaps permanently, damaged by the deportations and by other measures he had taken.

Nor was it just Rabin and his experts who were making such miscalculations. Ehud Ya'ari, one of Israel's most respected commentators, wrote in a column in the *Jerusalem Report* (1/14/93): "The waves of arrests over the past five years have undermined Hamas' attempt to build a solid underground. It retains a reservoir of support, but a few isolated cells are all that remain of its secret military network....There are even signs that it's retreating, with members leaving or keeping their distance."

From the perspective of twelve years later, years filled with dozens of suicide bombings, and continuous Hamas attacks and mass demonstrations, one can only say, *Halevai* (if only) what Ya'ari had written was correct.

What Arafat's speculations suggested to me was the painful extent to which Israelis and Palestinians alike didn't understand each other. Not in the least. What had really happened was that Rabin had committed an error that was now being explained by Arafat as a deeply calculated maneuver. But this, of course, was wrong. Whatever Rabin's feelings toward the PLO might be, the last thing in the world he wanted was to strengthen the hand of Hamas. What he had done to the Hamas leaders was not part of a maneuver against the PLO, but an act of rage against Hamas, who had just carried out the cold-blooded murder of an Israeli soldier. Rabin wanted both to punish the people responsible for such behavior, and damage their organization. And although I believed Rabin miscalculated in his assessment of what his policy would accomplish, he, and indeed most Israelis at the time, believed that these aggressive security measures were working.

Arafat, though, kept going on with what I believed to be a wrong-headed cynicism, arguing that Rabin "wants to delay the peace process to see if he can strengthen his hand."

Wayne tried to put a more positive spin on the deportation: "Suppose Rabin did it to provide political protection to permit him to make peace with the PLO?"

Abu Mazen, who was at the meeting and dinner, retorted, "I do not believe he signaled a right turn to make a left."

Wayne, concerned that this episode could end the possibility of finding a way to bringing Arafat and Rabin, or at least their representatives, together, asked Arafat, "Do you still want to pursue negotiations through the back channel if it's authenticated?"

"Yes. Definitely," Arafat answered.

Abu Mazen reassured us as well that the deportations, though regrettable, would not end the peace process.

At the meeting's end, an unusual exchange occurred between Wayne and Arafat. The Palestinian leader rarely spoke about his personal life, but he had been married two years earlier, and Wayne asked him, "Do you enjoy married life?"

"No," he said. "I don't get any time to enjoy it."

Wayne went on to note that Arafat was permitted by Islamic law to have several wives—as had formerly been the case with the Mormons—and that everyone knew that Arafat's marriage was to the Palestinian movement.

"Yes," he answered. "We are permitted to have four wives. The first three are the movement, and the fourth is my new one."

The joking helped the atmosphere, and we certainly left the meeting feeling a lot better than when we arrived. I thought of my earlier fears that maybe it would have been better had we not come, and realized yet again that meeting and talking is almost always better than silence and withdrawal. Arafat might have some strange, and very uncharitable, misconceptions about Rabin's motives, but it was important to get together and reaffirm that while the deportations had slowed down and hurt the peace process, they had not killed it. And as long as the peace process was alive, there was hope.

During the ensuing four months of the halt in official negotiations, a wave of clandestine talks began. It was becoming increasingly clear to Rabin that the current structure for the talks—dealing only with Palestinian leaders who were not in the PLO, but who had to clear everything they said with the PLO—was just forcing the sides into repeated deadlocks. And these deadlocks, and general lack of movement with the Palestinians, were holding back the possibility of making progress with the Arab states such as Jordan. Thus, even though King Hussein had pretty much ironed out a deal with the Israelis within the first couple of meetings, he refused to be the first Arab state to now reach a peace agreement with Israel. Fifteen years earlier, President Sadat had gone that route (settling with Israel before Israel had settled with the Palestinians), and the entire Arab world had jilted both Sadat and Egypt. Three years later, Sadat was assassinated. Now, King Hussein did not want to run that risk. Given the fact that over half his public was of Palestinian descent, he could not be seen as cutting a separate peace with Israel. If Israel wanted to make progress on the Jordan front, it would first have to make some settlement with the Palestinians.

It was against this backdrop that in December 1992, Israel finally removed the legal edict barring Israeli citizens from meeting with PLO members. During those first months, at least four back channels, operating through four intermediaries, were opened between Israel and the PLO, but most of these contacts ended after an initial meeting or two, without any headway being made. But then, one unlikely group gained some traction.

Two Israeli academics, Ron Pundak and Yair Hirschfeld, met with Ahmed Qurei, known as Abu Ala, the finance minister of the PLO, in a London hotel (it was at around the same time as Wayne's and my trip to Tunis). When Abu Ala insisted after the first get-togethers on broad negotiations with an official delegation, Hirschfeld called Yossi Beilin, Shimon Peres's deputy and Hirschfeld's closest contact in the foreign ministry, and Beilin, who knew the two men well, gave them permission to explore their new relationship with the PLO minister. As Pundak described it, Beilin gave them "a very long leash," in effect, carte blanche to explore all possibilities, and to report back at every stage of the contacts. This was the genesis of the now-famous Oslo Accords.

The talks with Abu Ala, which had originated in the London hotel, quickly shifted to Oslo—right after the Israeli ban had been lifted—where they continued in great secrecy and with the help of the Norwegian authorities.

Before committing themselves deeply to the negotiations, the Israelis—who had little information about Abu Ala—wanted reassurance that he had real power within the PLO. He soon provided it. Abu Ala claimed that he controlled several of the Palestinian delegations dealing with Israel in the official track, and he arranged for those delegations that had been making no progress to loosen their positions during the multilateral negotiations in Washington. Peres and the Israeli leadership immediately realized that Abu Ala was for real.

But now Abu Ala came back with a demand. It was not enough for him that the Israeli Foreign Ministry had supposedly authorized these two academics to speak with a PLO representative. He needed to know how real and deep were their ties within Israeli officialdom. Having demonstrated his credentials, Abu Ala now insisted during the spring of 1993 that Hirschfeld and Pundak do the same; that May, he threatened to halt the meetings unless an Israeli official joined the talks.

Peres was anxious to see this happen, Rabin was not; but finally, with Rabin's reluctant consent, Peres dispatched Uri Savir, director general of the Foreign Ministry, and Joel Singer, a lawyer who had worked on accords with Egypt, to join the two academics in the negotiations. From that point on, progress started happening very quickly. When Wayne saw Peres just three months later, in August, Peres told him that he thought a real breakthrough would be coming soon in the talks with the Palestinians, which would lead to the Palestinians gaining autonomy in Gaza and Jericho. Though Wayne obviously thought Peres was referring to the Washington talks with Faisel Husseini and Hanan Ashrawi—which had, until now, been unproductive—Saeb Erekat, who met with Wayne a day later, also indicated that something was brewing with autonomy in Gaza and Jericho, but "how, and what will occur, is not clear."

Just four days later, Peres flew to Stockholm, to meet secretly with Abu Mazen, the PLO foreign secretary, and to initial the Oslo Accords.

In September, Arafat—who had been banned from the United States since his "guns and olive branch" speech at the UN in 1974—arrived in Washington. Rabin and Peres came as well for what proved to be one of the momentous events of the Clinton presidency, the signing on September 13, 1993, of the Declaration of Principles (generally referred to as the DOP) by Arafat and Rabin in front of a deeply moved American president. The table on which the document was signed was the same one used by Begin and Sadat to sign the Egyptian-Israeli peace treaty in 1979.

Rabin, normally a man of few, and unemotional, words, spoke that day with great eloquence: "We, the soldiers who have returned from battle stained with blood... we, who have fought against you, the Palestinians, we say to you today in a loud and clear voice: 'Enough of blood and tears! Enough!'" Arafat replied in Arabic: "Our two sides are awaiting today this historic hope, and they too want to give peace a real chance."

Rabin and Arafat even shook hands, although it was clear that Rabin was uncomfortable doing so. In fact, as soon as he finished, he turned to Peres, and said, "Now it's your turn," the clear implication being that it was a dirty job, and Peres should do it and get it over with. Peres, however, did not seem at all upset at the thought of shaking Arafat's hand, and did so with more enthusiasm, and for far longer, than Rabin.

Wayne and I were in the audience of Americans invited to the White House–sponsored event, and we watched the proceedings in delight and with amazement. We realized that our almost five-year, on-again, off-again role as emissaries between Arafat and the various Israeli prime ministers and/or foreign ministers was over. From now on the sides could talk to each other directly. It occurred to us that there might be times when we would still be needed, to help smooth over tensions that might arise in the still far-from-complete negotiations.

Under the agreement signed that day, the PLO was given self-rule in Gaza and, as they had insisted, in Jericho as well. The Palestinians would become responsible for health, welfare, taxation, and other civil responsibilities in the areas under their control.

The agreement was also intended to encourage economic development in the West Bank and Gaza. To achieve this, an Israeli-Palestinian Economic Cooperation Committee was established to work on issues such as water, electricity, finance, transport, and communications. The Israelis were well aware that the economic viability of the newly handed-over portions of the territories would largely determine the success of the agreement. If the Palestinians saw real gains in the quality of their lives, their willingness to live in peace with Israel would greatly increase.

But even amid our joy that day, we realized that only a part of our job seemed to have been finished. For while what was happening with the Palestinians was being greeted with enthusiasm in much of the Arab world—for example, all six of the wealthy Arab governments in the Gulf publicly endorsed the deal—Hafez Assad was not enthusiastic. The fact that the Accords had been achieved through secret negotiations signaled to him that

Rabin intended to circumvent the American-sponsored peace process that was started in Madrid.*

But of course what was really behind Assad's lack of enthusiasm for the Oslo Accords was something else. Any agreement reached anywhere between Israel and any of her neighbors that did not hasten the return of the Golan Heights to Syria constituted in his eyes an irrelevant, even backward, step.

And, of course, Assad was not the only Arab figure to be hesitant about Oslo. Militant Arabs throughout the Middle East saw the accords in even more negative terms, as a betrayal of the sacred obligation of Muslims to destroy Israel. The radicals' target was not just the post-1967 West Bank settlements, but the entire state. The existence of Tel Aviv as a Jewish city was no less offensive to the Arab rejectionists than the Jewish settlement in Hebron. Early that September, shortly after news of the agreement was publicized—but before the Arafat-Rabin signing—twelve Palestinian and Islamic groups announced in Lebanon that they would work together to defeat the Accords.

There was of course nothing Wayne and I could do to appease the insatiable appetites of the extremist Palestinian and Islamic groups that wanted Israel dead. There

---

* It is not widely recalled today that even the moderate regime in Jordan was angered at learning that secret negotiations had been carried out simultaneous with the formal peace talks being held in Washington; Jordan certainly expected to be informed and consulted about any negotiations taking place regarding Israel and the Middle East.

was nothing Israel could offer them short of the Jewish state committing suicide.*

The same, however, did not apply to Assad and Syria. His rejection of Israel had been tempered by his loss of a Soviet patron and the reality of Israeli military might, and had less to do with ideology and religious extremism than with geography. Israel had something of his that he wanted back, just as he had something—a willingness to recognize Israel—that Israel wanted. As long as two sides have something that they want from each other, it's worth talking.

Clearly, our mission had not yet ended.

---

* At the same time, of course, there were no shortage of Israeli "rejectionists" who opposed the creation of a Palestinian state, and they vigorously denounced the Oslo agreement. The extremists in this camp started speaking of Prime Minister Rabin as a "traitor," thereby helping to create the hateful climate that set the stage for his assassination.

FIVE

The Elusive Pursuit of
Peace with Syria

For most of his time as prime minister, Yitzhak Rabin was far more concerned with reaching an agreement with Syria than with the Palestinians. It sometimes seemed as if Rabin saw the Palestinians as more of a nuisance than a threat. True, they carried out frightening, and occasionally horrifying, terror attacks, but there was no way they could mount a credible threat to Israel. In contrast, the Syrians had chemical weapons and a large supply of missiles.

The problem was that any accommodation with Syria would require Israel to give up the Golan Heights, the high grounds from which Syria marksmen, prior to the 1967 War, used to fire down upon Israeli farmers in the valley. Mention the Golan to Israelis, and almost everyone had the same response: an image of Syrian troops shooting at Israeli kibbutzim, and kibbutz children growing up in shelters. Even Ben-Gurion, who in his later years turned into a dove, advocated returning all the lands captured in 1967, except for Jerusalem and the Golan Heights.

Rabin, a military man his entire professional life, was as aware as anyone of the Golan's strategic significance. Most important, as long as Israel held on to this territory, any Syrian tanks sent to attack Israel would have to fight an uphill battle. Also, the listening posts Israel had set up in the Golan provided her with easy access to much Syrian intelligence.

On the other hand, Rabin was equally aware that the Golan did not provide Israel with quite the level of security claimed for it by the country's hawks. After all, Israel was in possession of this land in October 1973, and this had not prevented Syrian troops from streaming over the Golan Heights during the Yom Kippur War.

So what to do?

Hold on to the Golan and never have peace with Syria, or return it, and then run the risk of President Assad, or some future Syrian leader, reneging on the agreement and once again using the Heights as a weapon against Israel.

Unfortunately, the one option that would have best satisfied Israel's concerns was not available: return the large majority, but not all, of the Golan. For one thing was clear: If Israel wished to secure any sort of peace agreement with Syria, Rabin would have to do no less than what Prime Minister Menachem Begin had done to secure an agreement with Egypt: return every inch of land conquered in 1967.* If Israel did so, it could insist, as it

---

* The difference of course was that returning the Sinai in its entirety to Egypt posed much less of a threat to Israeli security than returning the Golan Heights to Syria did.

had done with Egypt, on peace, diplomatic relations, and security provisions. But if Israel insisted on holding on to even a small part of the Golan, there would be nothing to negotiate.

I had long known this to be the case, for, from our very first meeting several years earlier, President Assad had made it clear that when it came to "land for peace," the deal had to be all or nothing. In his rather homespun analysis—as I noted earlier—if a man breaks into your house, steals a work of art, and then says he won't return it until you pay him for it, do you do so? Of course not. The man is a thief: Let him return the stolen property and be happy if he doesn't go to jail. Similarly, let Israel return the "stolen" Golan first, and then Syria would be willing to consider, with no guarantees, the issue of recognition.

Very different analogies could of course have been used to counter Assad's. Such as, if a man threatens you with a gun and you overpower him, are you morally required to return the weapon to him, particularly if he's not even willing to guarantee that he will never threaten you with it again? Of course not, yet between 1948 and 1967, the Syrians had used the Golan Heights as a weapon—just like a gun—against Israel. Even worse, Syria, working in conjunction with Egypt, had provoked the 1967 War with Israel. In the days preceding the war, Assad, then the Syrian defense minister, had declared: "I, as a military man believe that the time has come to enter into a battle of annihilation." With such a background, he hardly seemed the right candidate to deliver moral critiques of Israel.

Nonetheless, Rabin, in his long-term desire to secure peace treaties with the surrounding Arab nations, told

U.S. mediators that he was ready to float a "hypothetical" to Assad, offering to return the entire Golan in exchange for peace and security guarantees for Israel.

Assad expressed openness to Israel's proposal, but accompanied his openness with the inevitable conditions. Rabin in turn was put off by Assad's demands. For example, Rabin insisted on "normalization"; that is, Israel would engage in a limited withdrawal from the Golan to be matched on the Syrian side by diplomatic ties, so as to "test" if the Syrian-Israeli relationship was working. Once Syria passed such a test, Israel would be willing to undertake a large-scale withdrawal over a five-year period. This demand, so vital to Rabin and the Israeli negotiators, was deemed offensive and patronizing by the Syrians: "You are not teachers and we are not pupils," was the Syrian response. Assad also rejected Rabin's demand for public negotiations.*

On both these issues, I don't believe Rabin was just being stubborn. He wanted to be sure that if Israel returned the entire Golan, it would end up with genuine peace. He also wanted to help build political support within Israel for the controversial act he was undertaking; many, if not most Israelis were frightened at the thought of giving back the Golan Heights to Syria. That is also why normalization, and public negotiations, mattered so much to him.

Shortly thereafter, during a period when there was a sudden surge of progress in Israel's negotiations on the Palestinian front, Rabin decided to draw back from the Syrian negotiations.

But that February—it was 1994—all hell broke loose. Dr. Baruch Goldstein, a resident of Hebron and a fol-

* See Itamar Rabinovich, *The Brink of Peace*, pages 154, 236.

lower of the late Rabbi Meir Kahane, walked into the Tomb of the Patriarchs in Hebron and opened fire during a Muslim prayer service, killing twenty-nine Palestinians. Israeli society was horrified by, and unequivocally condemned, Goldstein's act. At the forefront of those denouncing Goldstein (who was killed by Arabs at the scene) was the prime minister himself: "As a Jew, as an Israeli, as a man and as a human being, I am ashamed at the disgrace imposed upon us by a desperate murderer. You are a shame on Zionism and an embarrassment to Judaism."*

Unfortunately, such condemnations made little impression on the Arab world, many of whose members preferred to act (and maybe they weren't acting) as if Israel and its leaders approved of what Goldstein had done. There were mass anti-Israel protests all over the Arab world and within a few weeks Hamas and Islamic Jihad were carrying out terrorist reprisals against Israel. Eventually, the protests subsided, but not the terrorism. In the coming months, Hamas attacks escalated. On October 19, a Hamas bomber boarded a crowded bus in Tel Aviv and carried out the worst terrorist attack against Israel in sixteen years. Twenty-one Israelis and a visitor from Holland were killed.

But dominated as the Middle East tends to be by bad news, something good happened that month as well, something that made peace advocates a bit more hopeful

---

* Without of course in any way justifying Goldstein's attack, it should be noted that a few weeks earlier the son of a close friend, who had been fatally wounded by Arab attackers, had died in his arms. Also, on the day of the attack, reports circulated that Jews visiting the Tomb had been heckled by Palestinians with cries of "Death to the Jews."

that some good could be accomplished on the Syrian front as well. On October 26, 1994, Jordan became the second Arab country to sign a peace treaty with Israel. That this was not going to be a cold peace was suggested by a widely commented-upon event that had occurred just a few days earlier at the initial draft signing ceremony. Shimon Peres, Israel's foreign minister, embraced King Hussein and then kissed him on both cheeks.

Of course, this peace had been a lot easier to achieve than would be the case with either Syria or the Palestinians. Because Jordan had years earlier given up any claims to sovereignty over the West Bank, there were only a few minor territorial issues with which Israel and Jordan had to deal. Perhaps that's what enabled the king to declare that day, "This is a peace with dignity. This is peace with commitment. This is our gift to our peoples and to generations to come."

I was profoundly moved by Hussein's words. The man, as I knew from my meetings with him, exuded graciousness. In fact, an incident that happened a few years later just confirmed—on a very public scale—Hussein's profound humanity. In March 1997, a Jordanian soldier shot and murdered seven Israeli schoolgirls, aged thirteen to fifteen, while they were on a field trip to Jordan's "Island of Peace," near the northern border between Israel and Jordan. The devastation felt in Israel was overwhelming, and huge numbers of people attended the seven funerals. As more information about the dead girls emerged, the sense of bereavement deepened; it came out, for example, that one of the girls, Adi Malka, knew sign language and was her deaf parents' primary link to the world.

But then, on the day following the funerals, King

Hussein came to Israel. He went to the homes of each of the grieving families, got down on his knees, and begged forgiveness on behalf of his people. "I feel as if I have lost a child of my own," he said. "If there is any purpose in life it will be to make sure that all children no longer suffer the way our generation did." Even after the visit, Hussein stayed in touch with some of the families until his own death two years later.

But now back to the unhappy topic of Syria, Israel, and the missed chance for peace. In the fall of 1995, about a year after the agreement with Jordan, American secretary of state Warren Christopher started flying back and forth between Syria and Israel, and it soon appeared that his shuttle diplomacy was bearing some—if not a great deal of—fruit. At one point, reports started circulating that Syria was hinting at establishing some form of diplomatic relations with Israel even before Israel completed withdrawal from the Golan. But the breakthrough still didn't seem to be coming.

That October, Wayne and I met with Dennis Ross at the State Department. Ross was concerned that posturing by both Assad and Rabin was creating a stalemate. "Neither is feeling a sense of urgency, so nobody will do anything." Worse, "both sides think movement indicates weakness." If anything was going to be achieved, Ross argued, both Syria and Israel would have to be willing to show some real desire to come to an agreement, and be willing to compromise.

What was particularly troubling, and puzzling to us, was Assad's tendency to suggest that he was anxious to settle this issue, and then to draw back. Did he have political problems at home? His behavior would seem to indicate that he did, but then again, we had no evidence to suggest that this was the case. And like most dictators who had been in power for decades, he seemed pretty firmly in control.

On the face of it, it was clear to all three of us what each side needed from the other. Assad needed to get back the entire Golan, while reaching an accommodation with Israel that didn't compromise, or even appear to compromise, Syria's sovereignty. As Ross put it: "Assad wants security arrangements that permit him to say that the agreement doesn't impinge on Syria's sovereignty." That's why he was so adamant, for example, in opposing Israel's demand to maintain ground stations on the Golan.

Israel, in turn, needed a peace agreement, accompanied by guarantees of security adequate to assure Israel's fears about relinquishing the Golan. Any agreement that didn't provide for such guarantees would make it impossible for Rabin to sell such a plan to the Israeli public and, for that matter, to himself. And he needed to do both. Rabin had made it clear that he would not turn over the Golan to Syria without first presenting the plan to Israeli voters for their approval, and Rabin was not going to present any plan to Israelis that he himself was not sure guaranteed Israel's security.

It now became apparent why Ross wanted to speak with us. If no progress could be made between the Israelis and Syrians over the coming days, he wanted Wayne and me to do something that he could not: Go to Syria and convey to Assad that Rabin had no more than a fifty-fifty chance of winning the Israeli election that would be held in another year. If Rabin and Labor lost, then the Likud Party, headed by Benjamin Netanyahu, would come to power, and the likelihood of Syria getting back the Golan—certainly the entire Golan—would become nonexistent.

Ross didn't need to explicitly tell us that for him, an American diplomat, to make his preference in an Israeli election so clear to a foreign leader was something he could not do. Therefore, he wanted Wayne and I, two amateurs who had Assad's ear, to tell the Syrian president that "we think Rabin can make a deal, but he needs to see something from you. He sees no movement on issues of substance. You won't let the military [of the two countries meet]. There's no sign you want something to happen."

Later that same day, I went with Wayne to the Syrian embassy to meet with Walid Moualem, Syria's ambassador to the United States, and tried to feel out his reactions to the mission we hoped to undertake in Syria. I saw no reason not to be direct: "It seems that the basis for an agreement between Israel and Syria is evident to everyone, yet it is apparently stalled. How can we be of help?"

Moualem, of course, saw the entire problem as caused by Israeli intransigence, specifically Rabin's unwillingness to commit himself to a full Israeli withdrawal from the Golan. At earlier meetings, Moualem told us, Syria had agreed that in return for a full withdrawal, Syria would, among other things, inform Israel before carrying out any troop mobilizations. In addition, Syria even had indicated its openness to Israeli usage of satellites, U-2s, and radar surveillance; she would, therefore, have access to all the intelligence she needed. But instead of accepting these Syrian concessions as adequate guarantees, Israel kept insisting on its need for ground stations in the Golan. And ground stations, a tangible symbol of occupation, were unacceptable to the Syrians. End of issue.

Moualem, well aware that what he told us could quickly be conveyed to Rabin, kept pressing the point. "Rabin is a logical man. If we offer the technology to permit a complete set of warnings, he should agree, and not insist on ground stations."

I took into account Moualem's arguments, but I didn't know how much success we could achieve with Rabin, and we certainly didn't regard ourselves as experts on security matters and early warning systems. We chose therefore to stay focused on the bigger picture, emphasizing to the ambassador that Syria and Israel alike had a great opportunity now. And what a waste it would be if they didn't find a way to move it along.

Before we left, Moualem assured me that Assad was ready to reach an agreement with Israel before the Israeli election. So I walked out of the meeting guardedly optimistic, and anxious to transmit his message to Prime Minister Rabin.

But then, just a few days later, on November 4, 1995, during a peace rally in Tel Aviv, Yitzhak Rabin was assassinated by a Jewish extremist, Yigal Amir. The assassin was part of a group of Israeli activists who regarded Rabin as a "traitor" (they used the term repeatedly at their rallies) for advocating territorial compromise on the West Bank and the Golan, and for approving the Oslo Accords.

Sixty heads of state attended Rabin's funeral, including Egyptian President Mubarak, who had never been to Israel, and King Hussein, who offered a stirring eulogy. Meanwhile, Rabin's death sent shock waves throughout Israeli society, and it was not at all clear what this meant for the peace process.

After I got over my own sense of shock and bereavement, it appeared to me that, if anything, the peace process would continue, and maybe even accelerate. For one thing, Rabin had been murdered because of his support for making peace, so to slow down the process after his death would seem to represent a capitulation to Amir and to the extremists. Second, with Rabin's death, Shimon Peres had become the new prime minister, and he was an even more enthusiastic supporter of the peace process than Rabin. Peres had often made it clear that he had every intention of pushing for an early agreement with Syria.

So Wayne and I pressed on. A month after Rabin's death, in early December, we flew to Egypt to meet with our old friend and Mubarak's national security advisor, Osama El-Baz; he had long mentored Wayne and me in ways to move forward a peace agreement with Syria. El-Baz now reiterated to us what Moualem had said in Washington, that Israel's insistence on ground posts in the Golan would scuttle the possibility of any agreement. But he also insisted that Assad was genuinely interested in making a peace agreement in the coming months.

We transmitted El-Baz's conclusions to Prime Minister Peres, emphasizing that "Assad very much wants to make peace with Israel and to do so quickly (before the elections)." We also passed on El-Baz's belief that negotiations should open quickly with two teams working in parallel, one on military issues, the other on everything else. He thought that Uri Savir, who had played so vital a role in bringing about the Oslo Accords, should represent Israel on the nonmilitary issues, and Walid Moualem, the Syrian ambassador to the United States, should represent Syria.

Three weeks later, two days after Christmas, Israeli and Syrian delegations opened negotiations in Wye River, Maryland. But despite El-Baz's insistence that

Assad was very interested in making a peace agreement, things did not go as well as Israel had hoped. Whenever Israel raised the issue of normalization of relations, including economic and diplomatic relations, cultural exchange, and cancellation of boycotts, the Syrians were evasive. It seemed that they were there for one purpose, and one purpose only: to get back the Golan Heights. Before the land was back in Syria's hands, or so it seemed, there was little else to talk about.*

But even so, it looked like some progress might be made. Indeed, the second round of talks at Wye began on January 2, 1996, and focused primarily on military matters. In a few days of negotiations, some, but not a great deal of, progress was made; most notably, the Syrian negotiators, obviously acting with Assad's approval, agreed to a more specific discussion of normalization of relations.

But then, on February 12, Peres announced that he was calling for early elections, to be held on May 29, instead of late October. Assad was furious. He knew that serious negotiations would be hampered by the electoral process; Peres would need to show himself strong before

---

* The Israeli chief negotiator with Damascus and top historian on Syria Itamar Rabinovich has offered an interesting insight into Assad's unease with the economic aspects of Peres's peace policy: "He found the notion of joint businesses as offensive intrusion: an Israeli involvement in projects in the Golan Heights would be interpreted as perpetuating its presence there, and denying him the chance for a full liberation of Syrian territories lost in 1967." Rabinovich quotes Patrick Seale, Assad's biographer: "Most Syrians would have seen such a settlement as exposing their society, nascent industries, cultural traditions, and national security to hostile Israeli penetration. For Assad, it would have made a mockery of his entire career" (see Rabinovich's book *Waging Peace*, page 287).

the Israeli electorate—particularly when confronting an opponent like Netanyahu—and that would make it hard, if not impossible, for him to be compromising in the negotiations with Syria.

On the last day of February, a third round of Wye negotiations opened, under the ominous shadow of a horrific bus bombing in Jerusalem three days earlier, followed within a week by two more bombings in Jerusalem and Tel Aviv. As Itamar Rabinovich, Israel's ambassador to the United States, and the chief negotiator at Wye, later wrote in his account of the Syrian/Israeli negotiations, *The Brink of Peace:* "The Syrian refusal to denounce the terrorist attacks made our continued stay at the Wye increasingly untenable, and finally led Peres to a virtual suspension of the negotiations on March 4."

From that point on, matters started to deteriorate. That same month, Hezbollah guerrillas stepped up attacks against Israeli troops in Syrian-controlled southern Lebanon, and then, in early April, Hezbollah sent twenty-five rockets over the Israeli border, injuring thirty-six civilians. IDF generals presented Peres with a plan to carry out an extensive series of bombings in southern Lebanon, a tactic intended to drive tens of thousands of refugees to flee to Beirut, and thereby force the Lebanese government to pressure Hezbollah to halt the attacks.

On that same unhappy day, Wayne and I met with Peres, and he asked us to go to Syria and tell Assad that he wanted to meet with him. Again, our status as amateurs would enable us to operate as "honest brokers" without any political leaders putting their or their country's prestige on the line. Also, Peres instructed us to emphasize to the Syrian president that he must reign in Hezbollah before the retaliations intensified.

The next morning we flew to Syria. Our first meeting there was with Christopher Ross, the American ambassador. We wanted to get his read on the situation before we met with any Syrian officials. Ross told us that Secretary of State Christopher had already tried to broker a Peres-Assad meeting, and that Assad had said, in Ross's words, "OK in principle, but not now. Not enough groundwork."

According to Ross, the problems between Israel and Syria emanated in large measure out of Peres's and Assad's very different negotiating styles. Peres, the expansive romantic, wanted Israel's relations normalized everywhere in the region (with at least fifteen Arab states), while Assad was "determined to preserve at all costs, Arab dignity and honor." In other words, Assad wanted to get his land back, but he had zero interest, for example, in discussions of a grand vision for broader Middle Eastern economic cooperation between Israel and her neighbors.

Ross also believed that Assad, at some level, feared for his life: "He doesn't want to get ahead of his people. He won't be a Sadat. While Assad is a dictator, he knows there are certain red lines he can't cross." But Ross felt that it was more than just an issue of self-protection. He told us that Assad and the Syrians saw themselves as the "nagging conscience" of the Middle East, and morally obligated to defend Arab interests. His concluding words, I remember, were, "Assad views peace as desirable, not essential."

When I asked him, "How can he be led to consider it essential?" he answered, "That is the key question."

That meeting, of course, didn't leave us overly optimistic, and when we returned to our room at the Damascus Sheraton, the situation only worsened. CNN was reporting that the morning edition of the *Jerusalem Post* quoted Peres as saying that Assad had agreed to

meet him, but that they had not worked out details yet as
to where or when. We knew immediately that such an announcement was going to infuriate Assad and the Syrian
leadership. Even more frustrating to us was the realization that the CNN story was a distortion of what Peres
had actually said. Wayne and I had woken up that morning in Israel, so we had read the *Post;* fortunately, we had
also brought it with us. All that Peres had said was that
"in principle they [the Syrians] had agreed to meet with
us but we've got a lot of other problems to solve." Unfortunately, CNN had condensed Peres's words to make
them more sensational (i.e., that Assad had agreed to
meet with him) and therefore more irritating to the Syrians. And it's not as if the *Jerusalem Post* was available at
Damascus newsstands to correct the misinformation.

Shortly thereafter, we left the hotel for our meeting
with Foreign Minister Faruq Al-Shara, where Wayne and
I did what we could to emphasize the gains that could be
achieved by a Peres/Assad meeting. I remember I told
Al-Shara: "From my conversations with the President
[i.e., Assad], and my close acquaintance with the prime
minister, including dinner last night, I know the two of
them could come to some initial decisions if you could
get them together. I know the two of them could make
peace." And then, even before Al-Shara responded to
this statement, I mentioned Peres's second request, to
ask Syria to do whatever it could to stop the violence in
southern Lebanon.

Al-Shara ignored the latter point—as he would continue to ignore it throughout the meeting—and raised,
with some annoyance, Peres's claim that Assad had
agreed to meet with him. We showed him the *Jerusalem
Post* interview, and he read it carefully. I remember sitting there quietly for a full eight or nine minutes as he

perused the article. Unfortunately, when he looked up, it was clear that he was still not going to throw his support behind a Peres/Assad get-together, and I could only imagine that Assad had made it clear to him that he did not want such a meeting.

But now it was Wayne who chose to push the issue. He quoted something Uri Savir, Israel's chief negotiator with the Syrians and the Israeli architect of the Oslo Accords, had told us the preceding day: "Tell them that President Assad is making a mistake not to meet with Peres, and in seeing such a meeting as a concession. It is not a concession to meet with Peres, only a chance to size each other up."

Even though Al-Shara tried to remain pleasant—"We are always glad to see you. You are always welcome"—it was clear that we were not making any headway. At one point, as we pushed our agenda, he said, "You can't dictate to us." Shortly, thereafter, the Syrian bitterness about Peres's call for early elections came out: "He started off by saying that there would not be early elections, that he would rather lose the election than lose the chance to make peace with Syria." But then Peres had gone ahead and called for early elections. So what was the point of asking President Assad to meet with him? Why should Syria take seriously Peres's claims that he wished to make peace?

Things of course were not quite as simple as Al-Shara was depicting them. In truth, as we explained, Warren Christopher had been quite negative about Syria's commitment to an early agreement, and hearing the secretary of state's, and others' assessments, Peres concluded that it made more sense to get an early mandate from the Israeli public and then proceed with the negotiations. That was the real reason Peres had called for early elections.

There was nothing more that Shimon Peres wanted, we assured him, than to make peace with Syria.

I thought maybe I could push again. "It is a mistake for Peres and Assad not to meet. They could meet and make peace."

But Al-Shara was very concerned about protocol and process. "If you want to make a deal between major companies, you first have the others [the underlings] prepare the groundwork before the heads meet."

We had now shifted to more familiar ground, business negotiations, and here I felt I was on surer footing than Al-Shara, or Wayne, for that matter. One thing I had long ago learned in business negotiations: if you want to move things forward, you get the people who have the power to make decisions together. As I now told Al-Shara, "The big business deals in the United States are made by the chairmen, presidents, or the owners."

Wayne stepped in and backed me up, citing an example that he knew would not endear him to Al-Shara, but that proved our point: Sadat's trip to Jerusalem. As Wayne put it, Sadat's coming to Jerusalem in advance of negotiations by underlings is precisely what made certain that a peace would be negotiated." Even more important, from the Syrian perspective, it also brought about the return of all the land Egypt had lost in 1967.

But Al-Shara again ignored us, and instead turned to the situation in southern Lebanon, focusing on the Israeli bombings there. But when we again asked him to help hold down the Hezbollah attacks there—which would, of course, result in an end to retaliatory bombings by Israel—he suddenly moved in an altogether different, and surprising, direction. "And Netanyahu is giving more positive statements about Syria than Peres is....Why is Netanyahu apparently more friendly than Peres?"

To this day, it is hard for me to believe that Al-Shara was being serious. Netanyahu was known for saying that he would not give back the Golan, and his supporters were precisely those Israelis who held up the banners at demonstrations insisting on Israel never relinquishing control there. Peres, on the other hand, had been saying for years that Israel had to give back the Golan, and had to give land back to the Palestinians, and he had been saying it long before such a position had become conventional wisdom even within the Labor Party. I could only assume that Al-Shara's mind had been made up prior to our meeting—there would be no Peres/Assad get-together, and Syria would do nothing to halt violence by Hezbollah—and nothing we would say would make an impact.

But Wayne, conscious of course that what we said would be reported to Assad, added—and I admired his guts for doing so—"Is there any politically feasible signal Peres could send which could bring such a meeting [between him and Assad] about?"

Unfortunately, by this point, Al-Shara, a leading Syrian hardliner, was back in propaganda mode. Everything was Israel's fault; the bombings were Israel's fault, the blowing up of homes, all these things were poisoning the mood in the Arab world. So there was no sense in having a meeting between Assad and Peres.

"Would it be possible for Wayne and me to meet with the president to discuss these issues with him?" I asked.

"The president is very, very busy at this time," Al-Shara replied, thereby ending any chance we had to convey Peres's message directly to the person who most needed to hear it.

We flew straight back to Israel, and that night—it was late—after eleven, we called Peres, and told him

*Dan and Ewa Abraham with President and Mrs. Clinton,
December 31, 1999: Greeting the new millennium with the Clintons, and
about a thousand people. That night, the president gave us an award for
our support of Americare.* Official White House Photo

Dan with Vice President Al Gore

Official White House Photo

The vice president honored us by coming to our synagogue for a Simchat Torah service. When the service concluded, he offered to drive me back to my home. I explained that I didn't drive on Jewish holidays, and so he walked with me.

Official White House Photo

With President Hafez Assad of Syria: Assad was consistent. He always repeated that the 1967 border was the legitimate line between Syria and Israel. If Israel would return to that border, he would make "a just, secure, and permanent peace." That was the message I took from Assad to Peres, and later to Netanyahu.

President Assad (second from left), *with Congressman Gary Ackerman, Wayne Owens, Syrian Foreign Minister Faruk Al-Shara, and Dan in Damascus, 1997: Amid all the talk about borders and peace, there were lighter moments too. President Assad started to refer to me as "Mr. Slim Fast." At this meeting, Congressman Ackerman joked to Assad that I made a fortune from people like him.*

Visiting a Jewish school in Damascus

Dan and Wayne on their first trip to the Middle East in 1988, with Israeli Prime Minister Yitzhak Shamir in Jerusalem

Congressman Wayne Owens: A man I grew to respect and love. Wayne was a highly moral and ethical person, and this deeply religious Mormon believed with all his heart and soul that the most important thing he could accomplish was to bring peace between the Jewish and Muslim people. MH Concepts

Dan, with Lily and Ariel Sharon, and Wayne Owens at a meeting in 1994. In 2002, a year and a half after Lily's death, Prime Minister Sharon inscribed the photograph to Dan.

With Ariel (Arik) Sharon: Probably the most moving conversation I ever had with Arik was shortly after his wife, Lily, had died, and he had become Prime Minister. He was visiting the United States and invited me to his hotel room. We spoke for over an hour. At the end, I asked him, "How can I be of help to you?" He replied: "Just be my friend. Just be my friend."

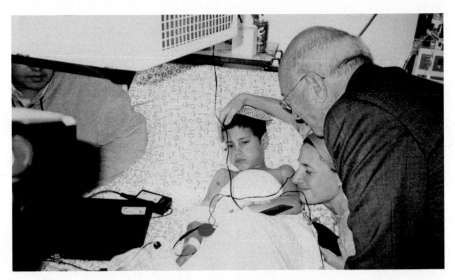

Dan at a hospital with a badly injured Israeli child and the child's mother: I went down to the hospital to visit a child whose feet had been blown off in a terrorist attack. What can I say, it was a very sad and heart-wrenching day.

With Shimon Peres: Shimon is one of my closest friends and a man of remarkable talents. He is always visionary, extraordinarily well read, yet full of life and fun. John Harrington

With Shimon Peres and Henry Kissinger: Sharing a light moment at a luncheon the Center for Middle East Peace held in Shimon's honor.

Sarah Merians

*Henry and Nancy Kissinger greeting King Abdullah and Queen Raina
of Jordan at the Center for Middle East Peace dinner at New York's
Waldorf-Astoria on their first visit to the United States as
King and Queen.*

Sarah Merians

Meeting with Israeli President Chaim Herzog at Beit Hanassi, 1985.
Chaim and his wife, Aura, were dear friends, and he honored our efforts
as well by attending the opening of the Center for Middle East Peace and
Economic Cooperation.

King Abdullah II of Jordan, with Congressman Sam Gejdenson (far left), *Bill Burns, Assistant Secretary of State for Near Eastern Affairs, and Wayne Owens* (far right)

Prince Saud Al-Faisal, foreign minister of Saudi Arabia, with Congressman Robert Wexler (left) and Wayne Owens (right)

The Emir of Qatar, His Highness Sheikh Hamad Bin Khalifa Al-Thani (right) and foreign minister, Sheikh Hamad Bin Jassim Al-Thani (left): The leaders of Qatar always made it clear that they were open to accepting Israel and to doing business with her.

Meeting with Crown Prince, and now King, Abdullah of Saudi Arabia:
The Prince repeatedly assured me that if Israel accepted the 1967 borders
as final, every Arab nation would accept Israel and live with her in
peace. When I told him that Israel couldn't give back everything, it
would need to hold on to some parts of the areas around Jerusalem that
had been built up, but that it would do a land swap to replace the areas
it was keeping, the Prince assured me that that would be acceptable.

Yasser Arafat: After a hundred lunches, dinners, and late-night meetings, it was clear that Arafat was the one man who could make something happen. And I could be direct with him. I told him: "Abu Amar, no Israeli government can sign a peace agreement that will allow the right of return of even one Palestinian. And there is no way Israel can turn over sovereignty of the Temple Mount to anyone except to the world." And yet, we always could talk.

With Abu Mazen and UN Mideast envoy Terje Roed-Larsen (left): Abu Mazen was always a gentleman, thoughtful, direct, and straight. He made it clear that he wanted to see peace achieved through two states for two people.

Dan and Ewa with Dr. Ephraim Sneh, Israel's Minister of Health, in Netanya, overlooking the Mediterranean Sea

Dan and Ewa in Aleppo: Is it any wonder that I love Ewa?

that we had not achieved anything significant. We didn't want to go into details over the phone—we had no idea who might be listening—and Wayne immediately typed up a six- or seven-page summary of the meeting; at 8:00 o'clock in the morning Shimon's aide, Boojie (Isaac) Herzog, picked it up. The most discouraging aspect of the report was not just that there would be no Assad/Peres meeting, but that on three separate occasions we had appealed to Al-Shara to help stop the Hezbollah attacks, and he had never responded to our plea, either to deny that the Syrians had such influence, or to promise to use it to prevent such attacks. He had just ignored our request, refusing to discuss it.

Later that day, after he had read the report, Peres called and told us how disappointed he was by the Syrian attitude. Forty-eight hours later, Peres gave the go-ahead and Israel launched Operation Grapes of Wrath, the massive attempt earlier proposed by the Israeli military to stop the Hezbollah attacks from Lebanon. For the first time since 1982, Israeli Apache helicopters flew right into Beirut and fired rockets through the windows of the Hezbollah headquarters. At the same time, Israeli ships sealed off Lebanese ports, and Israeli planes and artillery conducted devastating attacks in the south. Some 200,000 Lebanese villagers fled to Beirut, sparking a refugee crisis for the Lebanese and Syrian governments.

It was painful for us. It was one of those times when we felt like we had had the opportunity to do something. I couldn't help but wonder that if we had gotten in to see President Assad we could have prevailed upon him to meet with Peres, and everything could have been different. Instead, there would be no meeting, only more attacks, more bombs, more deaths, and, of course, no peace.

SIX

Netanyahu and Oslo

I had known Benjamin (Bibi) Netanyahu for fifteen years before he became prime minister, back from his days when he served in New York as Israel's ambassador to the United Nations. In those early days, our relationship was totally uncomplicated, since our politics pretty much coincided. But the change in my political orientation and an unfortunate incident that happened some time after he became prime minister almost destroyed our relationship.

In December 1998, Israeli president Ezer Weizmann had come on an official visit to the United States, and Wayne and I were invited to a small dinner in his honor at the White House. It was a high-profile event, with President Bill Clinton, Secretary of State Madeleine Albright, National Security Advisor Sandy Berger, and forty Jewish leaders from all over the country in attendance.

I was sitting between Albright and Berger, and what I most recall about the evening was that everyone kept pressuring the president to become more involved in the peace process. I was actually starting to find it annoying. Having one or two people express this hope to Clinton would have been all right, but you don't do it forty times around a table with everybody basically saying the same thing.

The responsibility for making peace between Israel and the Arab world is the responsibility of the prime minister of Israel and its people, and the responsibility of the leaders and people of the Arab countries. It's their future, it's their lives, and it's their responsibility to make peace or war. To put the pressure on someone else is, I believe, the wrong thing to do, when all the president was trying to do was to be helpful to the parties.

Our job is to stand behind the leadership and people of Israel in helping them to make peace, and to encourage the president in such an effort, but as everyone present that evening already knew, Clinton was already committed. Very much so. So, while all this was going on, I was sitting there thinking that there was more that Israel could do, and the Palestinians also. Then, Berger—I don't know if he was just intending to be provocative or thought he was being funny—whispered to me, "Netanyahu's got you guys in his hip pocket."

Unfortunately (and I don't say this with pride), but given that I was already feeling a bit provoked, I just turned to Berger, and said, "He's got us in his hip pocket, huh?" I then raised my hand and said: "Mr. President, we all know that you really want to make peace; you want to see peace come to the region. I've been traveling to the

Middle East since 1988, and I know that the Arab leaders want to make peace too. I even know Arafat probably wants to make peace. But do we know if Bibi wants to make peace...."

President Weizmann slammed his fist on the table and said, "Yes, he does."

By the way, Weizmann cut me off before I finished my comment. I was about to say, "because if he does want to make peace, there is more that he could do, and we would support that."

In any case, the story was picked up in the Jewish *Forward*, and Wayne predicted that that would be the end of our relationship with Netanyahu.

The irony of it was that I was no Netanyahu basher. I had spent months traveling around the Arab world trying to convince its leaders that Netanyahu was a man with whom they could make a deal. For example, when I went to Egypt a few months after the election, and saw President Mubarak, I found him in a rage at Israel and at Bibi. I was very discomfited since, from our earliest meetings, he had always displayed a calm demeanor. I remember I said to him, "I want to urge you to give Bibi a chance. He needs more time. I have known him for fifteen years, and I am sure that he wants to bring peace."

Mubarak rejected my words. He told me that he had given Netanyahu a chance, many chances. And what was he, and the Arab world, getting from Netanyahu in return? "Every day a new statement against peace." Mubarak told me that feelings in the Arab world toward Israel were reaching a new low. He recalled how, in the past, he had helped arrange meetings between Rabin, Peres, and King Hussein. But now, if he would try to propose a meeting between Arab leaders and Netanyahu, there would be no willingness to do so.

Osama El-Baz was present at the meeting as well, and what particularly irked both him and Mubarak was not just the coldness of Netanyahu's statements, but the expansion of Israeli settlements on the West Bank. El-Baz told us that Arafat had recently called him, crying, discussing the settlements.

Mubarak and El-Baz then started to speak of the slain Rabin and of Shimon Peres in a longing manner. It occurred to me that if Arab leaders had spoken of them with such affection when Rabin was prime minister and Peres foreign minister—and Israel had been willing to declare its permanent border then—we probably would have had peace treaties with all the Arab countries, and a Palestinian state as well. Now, they were telling me of how Rabin was flexible, and had kept every single promise he had made.

I understood their frustration with Netanyahu, but I wasn't fully buying it, either. I remembered my unhappy experience in Syria. Peres had been prime minister, and he was willing to return the Golan and make an agreement with Syria. At that time, he had asked two things from Assad. Would Assad meet with him? No. Would the Syrians use their influence to stop Hezbollah attacks against Israel from southern Lebanon? No. Instead, their foreign minister, Faruq Al-Shara, started lecturing Wayne and me on how it seemed to him that it would be easier for Syria to deal with Netanyahu than with Peres.

But then, as I said, I could also understand their frustration with Netanyahu. For one thing, his language was strident, and his manner brusque. I was reminded of that a few days later (December 22, 1996), when Wayne and I met with Arafat in Gaza. Arafat sounded desperate. He told us of how his top aides and advisors were trying to negotiate with Netanyahu's people and were being given the brush-off. "Just last week, my colleagues [including Saeb Erekat, the chief Palestinian negotiator with Israel] went to [Netanyahu's adviser, Yitzhak] Molcho to see him. Molcho gave them fifty minutes, and a day later an hour. "This is not negotiations," Arafat protested. As he understood it, either Netanyahu's advisors did not appreciate the importance of negotiating with the Palestinians, or had been instructed by the prime minister not to engage in any serious talks, but to cut short discussions before they became substantive.

I told Arafat of a dinner I had had with Netanyahu in a restaurant in Jerusalem some years earlier. I don't remember exactly when, but it was some years after his ambassadorship at the UN. What struck me that night was that Netanyahu did not come across as an ideologue but rather as very concerned with security. I remember how he took out a pen and drew a map for me, which I unfortunately lost, outlining a possible settlement with the Palestinians. I came away from the dinner definitely feeling that he was not opposed to a Palestinian state. I also remember that he said to me, "I will be the one to make the peace." I urged Arafat, as I had urged Mubarak, not to give up on Netanyahu. He wanted to make peace.

Three weeks later, my point of view seemed to be vindicated. The Israeli Knesset, obviously with Bibi's support, approved an accord—which had been reached earlier and had been agreed to in principle during Peres's time in office—that involved Israel giving up a part of Hebron. To the Palestinians, there was a brief

moment of excitement because a Likud government
was making territorial concessions. But the good feelings did not last very long. By mid-February, Israel was
preparing to start building 6,500 housing units on a
Jerusalem hill known to the Palestinians as Jebal Abu
Ghnaim and to the Israelis as Har Homa. To the Palestinians, so large a building project was yet more proof
that Netanyahu and his government would never make
any concessions on Jerusalem. And while the United
States vetoed a UN Security Council resolution con-
demning Israel's action, the General Assembly
condemned Israel by a 133-vote majority, which meant
that almost every country in the world that voted, voted
against her. In March, Arafat came to the United States
and gave speeches in which he stated repeatedly that
this housing decision might unravel all prior agreements
by the two parties.

A few days later, violent protests erupted in the West
Bank when Israeli bulldozers arrived at the hill. And
then, on March 21, a suicide bomber set off an explosion
in a Tel Aviv café, killing himself and three Israeli
women. Dozens more Israelis were injured. But Netanyahu was single-minded in going ahead with this Har
Homa building plan. The Oslo accord made clear Palestinian self-rule was to be focused in the West Bank and
not Jerusalem. Therefore, he had the right to do whatever he wanted within the city's limits. But I knew from
my own experience that it is not always wise to avail one-
self of all of one's rights. Particularly in so volatile a
situation, and particularly when Israel still had workable
relations in many areas with the Palestinian Authority.

From the vantage point of 2005, one can easily claim
that all the Palestinian security services are implicated ei-

ther in supporting, and certainly not suppressing, terror-ism against Israel. But in those days that was not the case. The Palestinian Authority, for example, was cooperating with Israeli security to bring down the networks that were responsible for anti-Israel attacks in the territories. And yet, what was Netanyahu's reaction when Israeli in-telligence services told him of the PA's efforts to combat terrorism? He declared that he knew better, that their in-formation was wrong.

But it wasn't. Indeed, after Palestinian police tried to subdue rioting throughout the West Bank at the end of March, Netanyahu's own defense minister, Yitzhak Mordechai, said: "I think the majority of the Palestinian forces' policemen were working with us against violence in the area."

We met the prime minister at his office on a Friday morning. Wayne was with me, as was Sara Ehrman, the senior advisor in our Center for Middle East Peace, and Congressmen Gary Ackerman and David Price. Ne-tanyahu was more keyed up than I had ever seen him. A tasteless article about his personal life had been pub-lished that morning in an Israeli paper, and it had clearly unsettled him. When he came into the room, he didn't even bother to say hello or shake our hands, which was totally unlike him. Instead, he went into lecture mode: "The central problem of Oslo was that we were to give territory in exchange for their pledge to fight terrorism. 250 Israelis have been lost because the Palestinian Au-thority didn't fight terrorism. In fact, there's been a quantum leap in terrorism. That's the equivalent of 10,000 Americans. They didn't carry out their side of the deal. And they didn't annul the Covenant."

This last was a reference to a provision in the PLO

Covenant calling for Israel's destruction, which the PLO had long promised to annul.*

Even though Israel had agreed to the Oslo Accords, nothing, Netanyahu made it clear, was going to induce Israel to give up defensible borders. And the Palestinian

---

* The Palestinian commitment to revise the Covenant or 1964 PLO Charter calling for Israel's destruction was first made in a letter from Arafat to Rabin written before the White House lawn ceremony of the Declaration of Principles, stating: "...the PLO affirms that those articles of the Covenant which deny Israel's right to exist are now inoperative and no longer valid. Consequently, the PLO undertakes to submit to the Palestinian National Council for formal approval the necessary changes in regard to the Palestinian Covenant" (*Letters of Mutual Recognition*, 9/9/93).

Over the next two years, Arafat reiterated on several occasions his commitment to convening the PNC to annul this provision of the PLO Covenant, and on April 24, 1996, Arafat did convene the PNC in Gaza to do so. The PNC reportedly voted to approve changes to the Covenant, and to appoint a committee to draft a new covenant incorporating these changes.

But while the U.S. and Israeli governments welcomed the vote, Netanyahu and others on the Israeli right argued that no specific anti-Israel clauses had been officially abrogated. Furthermore, no new Covenant had been drafted. After he was elected, Prime Minister Netanyahu argued that the failure to revise the Covenant violated the agreements made by the Palestinians.

In January 1998, while meeting with President Clinton, Arafat presented the president with a letter on the matter of the Covenant, reaffirming again that "All of the provisions of the Covenant which are inconsistent with the PLO commitment to recognize and live in peace side-by-side with Israel are no longer in effect." *(continued on next page)*

refusal to fulfill all of their obligations made him even less desirous of following through on the commitments made at Oslo. In addition, he was understandably irked by the PA's revolving door approach to arrests of terrorists. Just a day or two earlier, terrorists who had been involved in setting off a devastating bomb attack in Dizengoff Square had been released.

Congressman Ackerman was supportive of Netanyahu's angry outburst, telling him that he could think of numerous ways in which the PA had refused to comply with its obligations, and not a single way in which Israel had refused to do so. But still Ackerman did not want Netanyahu to give up on Arafat since the alternative, Hamas, would certainly be worse for Israel. "What must Arafat do?" Ackerman pressed him.

In response, Netanyahu did not get overly specific, focusing rather on Arafat's signing on to a credible plan to carry out his responsibilities. Which meant of course bringing about a reduction in and, ideally, an end to terrorism. In return, Netanyahu was willing to promise that Israel would work out a serious map, one that would grant the Palestinians an area with contiguous territory. He assured us that the decision he and the Cabinet would reach would be based on security considerations, not political ones.

On Thursday, December 10, 1998, the PLO Central Council met in Gaza and, by a vote of 81–7, reaffirmed Arafat's letter to President Clinton. The meeting became an international event, partly because it was attended by President Clinton himself. His presence was interpreted by the Palestinians as affirming U.S. support for statehood while viewed by Israelis as providing an imprimatur for the dissolution of the noxious old Covenant.

As he spoke, Netanyahu was scanning our faces, trying to assess our reactions. And then his emotions again went into high gear: "Just tell me one thing that I misled Bill Clinton about! Just one thing!" He pounded his palm on the table. "Who does he trust? Who would he rather buy a used car from, me or Arafat?"

We assumed the question had been rhetorical, but the prime minister remained silent, waiting for a response. Finally, Ackerman joked, "If it were up to me, I'd walk."

"And if you were the last shoe salesman," Netanyahu said, "I'd go barefoot." At least he was smiling.

But Ackerman, sympathetic as he was to Netanyahu's plight, would not let go. The crowd he was traveling with—I think that was the expression he used—was not going to be satisfied if he returned from this trip just telling them how much Netanyahu mistrusted Arafat. "They want to know if you want a deal."

"They're wrong [if they think I don't want a deal]," Netanyahu retorted. "If I wanted to abort Oslo, I could have. I've had limitless opportunities to abort Oslo." For example, he told us that he could simply have used the Fall 1996 violent riots at the Jerusalem Old City tunnel, in the aftermath of which fifteen Israelis had been killed with weapons that Israel had given to the Palestinian Authority, as proof that there was no Palestinian willingness to make peace with Israel and that, therefore, Oslo was null and void. But he hadn't done so. Instead, he reached an agreement on Hebron that the Cabinet and Israeli public could accept. "I was elected for two reasons: to stop terror and cut a deal for peace with which Israel can agree and which will also control terrorism. There were thirty-four terrorist attacks under the previous government and only two under mine."

After the meeting, we received a call from someone— I don't remember who—in the prime minister's office telling us that they wished to keep this dialogue with our Center for Middle East Peace going, but that it had to be off the record. That was fine with us; we had a good track record at keeping off-the-record meetings off the record. But from what we could gather, someone from the foreign minister's office leaked the story to the press. Within a day, the meeting was the subject of an article in *Ha'aretz:* "Bad Name for Used Car Salesmen."

Five days later, on December 17, we had a meeting with our second head of state on that trip, Syrian president Hafez Assad. By this time, a real rapport had developed between the two of us. He told me, I don't remember if it was on that day or on another visit, "Whenever you want to come, you are welcome. Even if you are in the air already, call me, and I will give you immediate landing rights, and welcome you." It never happened that I had so urgent a reason to see him, but if I had to, I certainly would have done so.

Anyway, despite Assad's generally grave demeanor, and his reputation for extreme stiffness —a reputation, by the way, that was inaccurate—his first comment to me was a combination gentle gibe and compliment: "I thought you were the Slim Fast man, but I see you have put on a little weight."

"I keep half of America slim," I told him.

At that point, Congressman Ackerman, who could afford to lose a few pounds, chimed in, "My weight predicament has been his fortune."

Assad went on to tell us that some twenty-five years earlier he had stopped exercising and soon saw that he had a huge belly. "I started to do two to three hours of exercise daily, every single day, and it was summer and I was sweating profusely. And yet I drank a lot of water as a specialist told me to do, and in less than a month I got rid of my strange belly." He had then installed a punching bag in his apartment. "But I never disturbed my neighbors. I took precautions. At any rate, no fighting, no punching today. We are working in diplomacy."

It seemed to me that Assad had provided us with a good segue into what we had come to meet with him about: "That is a good slogan. The fighting has stopped and you have quit punching. You are ready to make the peace."

Assad of course had his own take on the situation. Sitting ramrod straight as he always did, his elbow poised on the armrest, he picked up on my theme. "But now another boxer has come and we need to make sure that he is not punching where he shouldn't. We are very concerned that the new boxer wants to keep territory that is not his. The Israelis are saying 'peace' and now we're finding out that they don't want to make peace if it means giving up land conquered in war."

Now, Assad, like Mubarak and El-Baz, started to speak of Rabin and Peres in the most complimentary way. He spoke of how the two of them could discuss the most sensitive issues with third-party intermediaries "with logic and in a friendly atmosphere." And he noted that both Rabin and Peres agreed that all of the Golan would be returned, that Israel laid no claim to any of it. According to Assad, this concession alone constituted 80 percent of the Syrian/Israeli peace process; the only significant remaining element was security arrangements, and the negotiations had bogged down over the issue of early warning stations. He, however, had agreed that the United States could take satellite pictures and send joint reports to both Syria and Israel; therefore, there was no need for early warning stations. According to Assad, "If Israel hadn't called for early elections, the negotiations could have been finished in eight months."

But Netanyahu, Assad protested, didn't want to resume the discussions on the basis of the agreements that had earlier been reached. He just wanted to start the negotiations anew.

Congressman Ackerman pressed home the point I had tried to make a year earlier with Foreign Minister Al-Shara, "If you and the Prime Minister sit down, you can strike a deal."

And Assad responded as Al-Shara had a year earlier: "Negotiations don't start at the top level, they start at lower levels. Failure at the top is a serious problem."

He started speaking in a more musing and philosophical—but discouraging—manner: "We have been adversaries for thirty or forty years. We will wait. It is unreasonable to think that peace can be established if it is not a just peace."

We were moving in a direction I didn't want to go. I said to him. "You said we have time. I'm seventy-three. We won't live forever."

"You don't look seventy-three," Assad said.

"Slim Fast! But I'm getting older."

But then the joking ended, and Assad's grave demeanor returned. "I didn't say we're not in a hurry to reach peace, but if others are not ready, so we are not."

And with that the meeting ended.

The next morning, there was a picture of Assad and me on the front page of Syria's English-language newspaper. The congressmen were suspiciously absent. It didn't require a Sherlock Holmes to decode the message Assad was sending. He wanted no public connection to Netanyahu. But if Netanyahu wanted a quiet dialogue, then it should go through Wayne and me. In other words, he wanted us to transmit what he had said to the prime minister. This gave all of us who had attended the meeting a certain feeling of satisfaction. Our collective encouragement to Assad to communicate with Netanyahu had sunk in.

We immediately returned to Israel, and the prime minister invited me to his home. The two of us met alone in his living room, and the meeting got off to a relaxed beginning. Bibi loves cigars, and he was smoking a long Cuban cigar and clearly enjoying it. I summarized our collective take on the meeting with Assad: "He wants to make peace with you on the 1967 borders. He wants peace, but his price is the '67 borders."

"And why should I agree to the '67 borders before we start negotiating?"

I tried to draw an analogy; I don't know if it convinced him. I took a cup and put it on a plate. "You own a home. This cup is the home, and the plate is the borders around it. Someone wants to buy the house and the land around it. You have a house, the Golan Heights. He's offering to buy it from you. But he wants all of it. His price for peace is the '67 borders. What are you going to ask him for it? What is it you want?"

"In that case, I have fifty-five demands."

I had no way of knowing whether he was being metaphorical or literal, but since I always assume that when someone tells me something, they are telling me what they really mean, I took out my pen and pad. "Great! What are they?"

"Well, we have to have stations up on the Golan, listening posts."

I marked it down, and sat with pen ready, poised to

continue. But Netanyahu stopped short, and gave me a long, level stare. "What did you say to the president [Clinton] that night?"

Oh God! I thought that had been long behind us. "What's the difference?" I said to him. "We're talking about peace between Israel and Syria? Let's continue. We're on a good track here. I can go back tomorrow, and he'll see me tomorrow. Let's get this thing going."

"No," Netanyahu said. He was not letting go. "What did you say to the president, what did you say to him?"

"Whatever I said to the president, I thought would come out in a positive way. If I said anything negative, I deeply apologize from the top of my head to the bottom of my soles."

I thought I was being pretty abject, but it wasn't enough. He wanted to know my exact words, and finally I told them to him, including those deadly words: "But do we know if Bibi wants to make peace?"

"You said that?" Netanyahu said with real anger, and stormed out of the room.

Obviously, I was upset, and obviously I would never have said what I had said if I could have foreseen the consequences of my words. But I didn't feel totally disheartened, either. I remember the thought processes that started to run through my mind as I sat alone in his living room, and the thoughts that continued to dominate my thinking for the next few days. "He really wants to make peace with Syria. He knows what the price is. I think he started to figure that I had caught him and that's when he stormed out. But his instinct was to go forward. So I said to myself, okay, he wants to go forward, but he doesn't want me in the picture."

I waited in his living room a little longer. Finally, his

chief of staff came in and I asked if I could see the prime minister again soon. He gave a very noncommittal response. It was clear I was not in Bibi's good graces, and so I left.

When I came back to New York, I sought out Malcolm Hoenlein, the long-time executive vice-chairman of the Conference of Presidents of Major Jewish Organizations, and a highly respected figure in the American Jewish community. He was just the right person for me to outline my dilemma. I told him what had happened, then said, "I've got to believe that Bibi is interested in reaching an agreement with the Syrians, but he doesn't want to do anything with me. So I need to know who is his biggest supporter and the person he is most friendly with in the Jewish community." Malcolm gladly set up a meeting for me with Ron Lauder, a prominent philanthropist and conservative political activist from the Estee Lauder family, and a man who had served both as an American ambassador and as chairman of the Conference of Presidents. Malcolm told me that Lauder was a long-time backer of Netanyahu's causes, and had a close and ongoing relationship with him. I contacted Lauder and set up a meeting for the two of us with the Syrian ambassador in Washington, Walid Moualem, to help figure out what could be done to revive the peace process between Israel and Syria. At the meeting, Lauder pushed Moualem. He asked him the hard questions, but he was satisfied with Moualem's answers. Eventually, Lauder made nine trips to Syria, and went back to Israel to report to Netanyahu.

To the best of my knowledge, Israel and Syria came close to an agreement on the issues dividing them. But while Bibi was willing to make some territorial concessions, he was not ready to go back to the '67 borders, even if that could have led to a peace agreement.

Again, Syria and Israel had come close. Close, as Groucho Marx liked to say, but no cigar.

SEVEN

Barak, Arafat, and the Aftermath of Camp David

In September 2000, less than two months after the collapse of the Camp David talks hosted by President Clinton—an effort to achieve a settlement between the Israelis and the Palestinians—Prime Minister Barak and President Arafat found themselves in New York attending the United Nations Millennium Conference, a gathering convened to discuss the UN's role in the new century.

As is now well known, Arafat and Barak had not achieved good personal chemistry at Camp David. That, of course, is an understatement. Arafat and his negotiating team attributed the tension to what they claimed was Barak's cold and indifferent manner. According to them, Barak's proposals, and even his words, when set down on paper, sounded encouraging, but he made little or no effort to establish personal rapport with his adversaries; more often than not, he ignored Arafat and the PLO officials. During one of the dinners at Camp David, for example, he shaded his face with his hands, and remained silent. Indeed, so marked was Barak's coldness that, two months later, during the Millennium Conference, when the two men ran into each other at an elevator bank, Arafat turned to Nava Barak and said to her, "Mrs. Barak, who is that stranger standing next to you?"

Nonetheless, when Barak arrived in New York for the UN conference, he came with a request from President Clinton to meet with Arafat. Clinton hoped that a meeting between the two, in the aftermath of the Camp David collapse, could help revive the Israeli-Palestinian talks. Barak agreed to the president's request, but he wanted the meeting to be low-key, and definitely not publicized.

It was likely with that thought in mind that he called me when he got to New York and said, "Would you do me a favor and arrange a dinner with Arafat and myself?"

"I'll do my best," I told him. "I can't promise anything, but I'm seeing Arafat tomorrow night."

Wayne and I had dinner that next night with Arafat at the UN Plaza Hotel. We rented a suite there, and arranged for dinner to be sent up. There were others there as well, some of Arafat's aides, some of our good friends, including one of my very closest and best friends, and the head of detectives in New York, Wally Zeins, about fourteen people altogether. At one point during the evening, I took him aside, and said to him, "Barak would like to get together and have dinner with you."

Arafat immediately agreed, and I recommended doing it the following night. I emphasized that the meeting should be conducted in private, away from the lights of television cameras, and therefore suggested that both he and Barak be driven straight to the underground garage in my apartment building, from where they could take the elevator to my apartment; that way, it was unlikely that either of them would be seen, and the meeting could be kept quiet. Arafat agreed to everything I proposed, and I assumed we had a done deal. But when I called Barak to confirm the meeting, he backed out very emphatically, "No, no, no, too soon. We'll do it in Israel when we get back."

I assumed that everything had happened so quickly— he had requested my involvement only two days earlier—that he had not readied himself to meet Arafat just yet. I can only assume that Barak's feelings about such a meeting must have been ambivalent. In any case, he did assure me that he really wanted to meet with Arafat once he got home.

A few days later, Barak flew back to Israel, where, on September 19, he announced that he was suspending talks between Gilead Sher and Saeb Erekat, the respective heads of the Israeli and Palestinian negotiating teams. Barak explained that because of the "extremist" positions adopted by the Palestinians since Camp David, there was no point to continuing the talks. Erekat, in turn, consulted with Arafat, and then announced, "Israel...intends to leave the peace process. This is a deep crisis and we seem to have reached an impasse."

Realizing that his decision had put Israel in danger of being blamed for derailing the peace negotiations, Barak quickly issued a clarification, announcing that he was not suspending the talks, but that he wanted some time out for consultation. Clearly, Barak had been rattled. Three hours later, the prime minister's office issued the day's third announcement, that "Attorney Sher will meet with Saeb Erekat."

It was into this sort of discouraging atmosphere that Wayne and I arrived in Israel. The Israeli press was already calling the turn of events a mini-crisis for the prime minister, characterizing his behavior as amateurish zigzagging. My impression was that something altogether different was going on. Barak, I believed, simply wanted to soften up the Palestinian's hard-line negotiating stance in order to move the peace process forward. But the Palestinians, by criticizing Barak's behavior as indicating a lack of commitment to peace, had won the public relations battle, and forced him to backtrack.

In truth, the Palestinian position did play out well in the world. Subsequent to Barak's first announcement, Arafat had gotten on the phone with President Clinton, President Mubarak, and the leaders of France, Jordan, and Morocco, all of whom he knew would sympathize with his desire to keep the discussions going. But in the court of Israeli opinion—and to Barak this was the most important court—the Palestinian negotiator's increasingly militant positions were not playing well at all. For example, Abu Mazen's statement, in response to Barak's suspension of the talks, that the Palestinians would not be cowed by Barak's behavior and would not backtrack on the issues of Jerusalem, the refugees, and the settlements, played into the worst fears of the Israelis. Certainly, there are many Israelis—most in fact—who, in return for peace, will be willing for Israel to withdraw from the large majority of the settlements; and there are also many Israelis who are willing, in return for peace, to grant Palestinians sovereignty in Arab-dominated parts of Jerusalem, and certainly in the Muslim holy places. But any insistence that there would be no compromising on the issue of the refugees was a red flag to Israelis. If the Palestinians, who claimed to number four million, intended on insisting that Palestinians had the "right of return" to Israel, then, if Israel reached an agreement with the Palestinians, the country would face demographic suicide. The Jewish state would soon become an Arab state with a large Jewish minority.

Almost immediately upon our arrival in Israel on September 20, Wayne and I—aware of the new crisis that was looming—drove to Jerusalem to meet with the prime minister. Barak's manner with us was cool, even curt, but I did not take it personally; what seemed most obvious to me was that he was downcast. Therefore, I found it encouraging that he pressed us to arrange a meeting with Arafat.

That night, we met with Arafat in his Ramallah compound, known as the Muqata. It consisted of a courtyard encircled by buildings at the edge of downtown Ramallah, the central hub of the Palestinian government. We were met by Nabil Abu Rudeineh, Arafat's chief of staff. We followed him down the corridor to the main meeting room. Within a few minutes, Arafat entered the room along with Hassan Asfour, one of the negotiators of the Oslo Accords, and they both greeted Wayne and me with a handshake and a hug, as is the Arab custom when meeting friends.

Because I saw the situation now as pretty desperate, I did not want to, in any way, minimize the need for Arafat and Barak to take decisive actions. "Please take what I say in friendship," I began the conversation almost immediately upon our arrival. "I have always tried to be honest and straightforward. We have been visiting with you for thirteen years. We have this one real opportunity to make peace."

As Arafat himself acknowledged to me, with the White House involved in elections, and Barak's attention increasingly focused on domestic affairs, this might be the last chance for a long while to move the peace process forward.

And so I came to my pitch, the primary reason I had been so anxious to see him. "It's worth the whole thirteen years Wayne and I have traveled to meet with you and others. It will be worth it one hundred times over for you and Barak to meet. He has turned his people; peace is worth everything and he's put everything on the table. You should meet to tell each other your inner feelings. It has to be you and him and it has to be soon. He wants the peace as much as you do."

In addition to their having little chemistry between them, Arafat and Barak, I also knew, were temperamentally polar opposites. Had I made such a proposal to Barak, he would have thought it over for a few seconds, and given me an answer. Barak liked to make his decisions in isolation, and certainly without extensive input from others. I remember somebody once saying that "Barak's inner cabinet resides between his right and left ear." In general, he would make decisions before consulting his advisors and then, like the army commander he had long been, he would expect his subordinates to fall in line.

Arafat, in contrast, was garrulous but passive. He would consult with every faction on every decision, and each would pepper his plans with their own conditions. Frequently, no decision would end up being made.

So now, in response to my request that he meet with Barak, he hedged, "I will discuss it with my near friends, with Abu Mazen especially." I was encouraged, though, because it seemed clear that he was going to come back with a positive response. Within a few seconds, he was already suggesting that if the meeting occurred it should take place at Abu Mazen's house, in Ramallah. Barak, he noted, had been there three times already.

Arafat then shifted into autobiographical mode and,

here, I must admit, I have no way of knowing if he was telling the truth. He told me that, as a child, he had lived adjacent to the Wailing Wall, in Jerusalem's Old City. "Every day as a small, five-year-old boy, I danced there with the Jews. I went to visit and saw them pray." And, in a typical Arafat verbal flourish, he told me that he had told Dennis Ross and Ross's largely Jewish negotiating team: "I prayed there at the Wailing Wall more than any of you."

The truth is, Arafat's childhood is steeped in mystery. Although Arafat claims to have grown up in the Old City of Jerusalem, his birth certificate says he was born in Egypt; he insists that the Egyptian certificate was forged during his student days in Cairo, in order to obtain the same benefits as native-born Egyptians.

Now, having shared with us his autobiographical reminiscences about the Western Wall, Arafat went on to inform us that the issue of Haram Al Sharif (the Temple Mount) had to be faced squarely. Anything less than a full concession on this issue by Barak, which meant anything less than total Muslim control of the Mount, was insufficient. "Barak does not want to understand. The Haram can only be Muslim. This is the holy place for Muslims." He also added, whether it was precisely at this moment, or a short time later, that he could never compromise on the Palestinian right of return to Israel. And then he said, "Or they'll kill me."

I responded: "Abu Amar, that's the price of leadership."

He had never spoken like this before, and I sat there wondering: Was this just rhetoric, or did he truly fear his own people? And if he did, could he be the one to make the compromises necessary to bring them to peace?

As the conversation continued, it became apparent, once again, that the Palestinians and Israelis were inhabiting two different worlds, with very different world-views. Each side, for example, was convinced that it was they, not their opponents, who was being called upon to make the primary sacrifices. Thus, when Arafat now spoke of his willingness to let the Israelis continue to use the Jewish Quarter and the Western Wall, he sounded like a generous monarch who, out of the goodness of his heart, was willing to permit the Jews to retain sections of Jerusalem's Old City. Indeed, the PLO had long interpreted UN Resolutions 242 and 338 as obligating Israel to give up every inch of land conquered during the 1967 War. Therefore, Israel had no legal basis for insisting on any rights at all to control the Jewish holy places; he even brought out a document, dating to the time of the British Mandate, in which the British had written that the Western Wall should be under Arab control. Nonetheless, Arafat, out of his noble desire to show goodwill, was willing to make a sacrifice, and allow Israelis continued access to places such as the Western Wall.

The Israelis of course knew quite a different narrative. First of all, since Israel controlled the whole West Bank and all of Jerusalem, why should they have to rely on Arafat's generosity to continue to have access to Jewish holy sites? Rather, it was they, not the Palestinians, who since 1967 were acting generously by permitting Muslim religious authorities to administer the Temple Mount. In addition, the only reason Israel controlled the West Bank was not because she was an imperialist nation but because an Arab coalition of states including Jordan had provoked a war with them, and Israel had conquered the land in a war of self-defense. Furthermore, Resolution 242 did not oblige Israel to give back all "the territories" in exchange for peace. The resolution had specifically spoken of "territories," and the reason the word "the" had been left out of the resolution was to indicate that Israel had to return some, but not all, of the conquered territories. Israel's willingness, therefore, to pass some of the West Bank lands to Arafat and the PLO should be regarded as a huge sacrifice and a magnanimous gesture on her part.

But now I was starting to pick up on a new thread in the way Arafat and Asfour were defining the issues, and I must admit that what I was hearing was quite disturbing. Both men kept emphasizing the sacredness of Jerusalem to the Palestinians and to the Muslim world in general, but in a manner that made it clear that they thought that the Muslim claims to the city were the only ones that mattered. Essentially, they were ignoring any Jewish connection to the city and to the land; indeed, they seemed unwilling to acknowledge such a connection. "But it is sacred to Israelis too," I said, and then I became more emotional: "Jerusalem has been a holy city to the Jewish people for more than 3,000 years, and the Palestinian people need to be sensitive and respect the rights of the Jewish people to the city of Jerusalem. Very sensitive. You need to recognize that."

Wayne, who was sitting there with a long reporter's notepad recording each word, looked up in shock. Rarely, in all the years of our meetings, had he heard me speak with such emotional intensity. It was clear that the relaxed nature of the meeting had turned explosive. Arafat's lips were trembling, and his eyes had a glassy look to them.

At this point, Wayne, less emotionally involved than I was, tried to deflect the growing argument: "Isn't there a compromise to be had on the issue of sovereignty?"

"He [that is, Barak] opened the question of sovereignty, and made it public. So it can't be closed," Arafat said.

Asfour now stepped in to back up Arafat's position, arguing that Barak had been foolish to open up the issue of the Temple Mount at Camp David. "It was not the time to bring it up." Indeed, it had created a big problem for the Palestinians, because once the issue was raised, it was not a matter on which they could backtrack.

And then, Arafat, perhaps annoyed at how I had spoken, decided to raise the stakes once again, resorting to perhaps the most infuriating argument I had ever heard him use: "For your information," he now began, "recently there was the very important news that they found a temple excavated in Yemen. Experts did the excavations, not just Palestinians. This may be more important than the Pyramids. It will be a big story. Khamal Salibi, who was Lebanese, did a very important history about the Jews from Yemen. The Jews were living in Yemen for a long time and had an empire, actually." Arafat went on and on about this supposed "find," and it was clear that he was suggesting that the Jews had never really lived in Palestine, rather in Yemen. And that Yemen, not Jerusalem, is where the Jewish temple stood. The upshot of what he was saying was that what existed in the Old City of Jerusalem was an exclusively Muslim holy site. None of it, the Western Wall included, had anything to do with the Jews.

These sorts of arguments had become increasingly familiar material in Arafat's stock presentations. At Camp David, he had announced on the first day that Palestinian archaeologists had found no evidence at all of any Jewish presence in the past in the area of the Temple.

During my thirteen years of meetings with Arab leaders, I had gotten used to a certain protocol. Wayne and I would walk into a room, we would be greeted politely, but then, before any real conversation could take place, we would often be subjected to a withering thirty-minute monologue on how terrible Israel and Zionism were in their actions toward Arabs, along with a detailed depiction of the many wrong things Israel had done and was doing to the Palestinians. Needless to say, these monologues were usually filled with incorrect statements, half-truths, some truths, and exaggerations, and I, a committed Jew and a Zionist, was irritated by them. But I had long ago made a decision to exercise restraint and remain silent. The Arab leaders with whom I was meeting held the keys to a peaceful settlement of the Arab-Israeli conflict, and for me, peace was the only battle worth fighting for.

But this evening, I could not ignore Arafat's words. This was different. He was in the midst of serious negotiations with Israel, and while Barak and the Israelis were trying to show a level of sensitivity to Palestinian needs and desires, Arafat was now denying the most basic beliefs of Jews and Israelis. It was very discouraging and worrisome to me; people who wish to make peace don't deny the most basic facts about their opponent's history.*

---

* People sometimes ask me if Arafat believed what he was saying when he made these outrageous assertions. After years of dealing, often warmly, with Arafat, I am still not certain. Sometimes, I think that he so desired to believe certain things, such as that the Jews have no significant connection to the Land of Israel, that he convinced himself that what he wanted to believe was true, and then came to believe it in his heart.

Other times, I think there were different forces at work. Wayne and I saw another, equally disturbing example of how Arafat played with the truth during a discussion we had around this same time with Saeb Erekat. Arafat had directed the two of us to get together with Erekat and, at the meeting, Erekat started going on about how the Temple Mount must always remain in Arab hands, and that the Jews have no connection to it, and never did.   *(continued on next page)*

Wayne intervened, trying to head off what he knew could soon turn into a rancorous argument. Instead of going into the finer points of Jewish history, he talked

---

Wayne said to Erekat, "But how can you say that? Every Jew and Christian believes that that is where Solomon's Temple stood, and this is where the Second Temple was extended by King Herod. You and Arafat have to at least acknowledge that, and say it."

"He can't say that," Erekat said.

"But it's true," Wayne said. "Why can he not just say that he understands that this is a holy place to the Jews?"

"He can't say that," Erekat repeated over and over, his voice growing louder with each repetition.

A moment later, the large doors to the room pushed open, and Arafat entered with two or three of his people. "I think it's time to end the meeting," he said. "Saeb has to get up for a six in the morning meeting."

The meeting immediately adjourned, and it was assumed by both of us that Arafat may have been standing by the door listening.

And why, I wondered that night, couldn't Arafat, or Erekat for that matter, say those simple words. We weren't asking the Palestinians to give up any land or any Arab claim. All that the Israelis wanted was just to hear a simple acknowledgment that the land under dispute was also holy to the Jews.

Again, was it pure perverse obstinacy? An unwillingness to acknowledge that other people have dreams and holy places? I don't think so. Rather, I was told that Islamic teachings forbid building mosques over other people's holy places. Certainly, many Islamic rulers have done so, but according to Islamic law it is forbidden. For Erekat or Arafat to acknowledge that the Muslims had built their holy mosque on the site of the Jewish temple would call the mosque's very legitimacy into question. That is why Erekat kept saying, "He can't say that." He couldn't say it because to say such a thing is to delegitimize what had become a Muslim holy site.

rather of the upcoming U.S. elections in November, and the positive effects any diplomatic rapprochement reached now might have on the Middle East situation. As Wayne saw it, the new administration would be very open to offering a generous package to the Palestinians if a deal were signed. But he believed such a deal had to be signed soon.

Arafat and Asfour agreed with Wayne on the urgency of the situation, but they put the blame for the stalemate on Barak's shoulders, on his intemperate nature, and his take-it-or-leave-it style of negotiating. In addition, they really believed that Barak and the Israelis pretty much controlled the U.S. administration. Though America was the far stronger country, and was supposedly serving as an honest broker in the Israeli-Palestinian negotiations, it was the Israelis who, according to Arafat, told the Americans what positions to take, and it was the Americans who followed their orders. Arafat claimed that "When I sat down [at Camp David] with President Clinton and he started to tell me about his plan, I took his plan out of my pocket and gave it to him, and told him we had received it the day before from the Israelis. Look at my notes. Here it is."

Arafat pulled out a small notebook, and showed Wayne and me the notes from his Camp David meeting with the president. There were two pages, filled with very neatly written characters in Arabic, which, of course, Wayne and I could not read. And even if we could, what could they prove? That the Israelis had dictated to President Clinton in advance what positions he should take? I don't think so.

The meeting ended a few minutes later, and Abu Rudeineh walked us to our car. Upset as I had been at the tenor of the meeting, I was not yet willing to let go of the bigger picture. President Clinton would be out of office in a few months, and we had no way of knowing who would be heading the new administration. But of one thing I was certain. Whether it was Gore or Bush, neither one was likely to be as committed to forging a peace agreement between Israel and her neighbors as Clinton was. Therefore, I now said to Abu Rudeineh, "We have to get it done now, in the next few weeks, while Clinton can work on it."

To my relief, Abu Rudeineh did not start pitching polemics at me. "We know that. We understand that."

Still, I was frustrated that so little had been accomplished at this meeting. I emphasized again to him the importance of Arafat's meeting with Barak, and then we left.

Several things had bothered me about the meeting. Obviously, one of the more prominent was Arafat's attempt to show that Yemen, not Israel, was the ancient Jewish homeland. But I found that what bothered me most of all, the line to which my mind kept returning, were those three words, "They'll kill me."

In fact, for me those words constituted something of an existential crisis.

We had first met Arafat in Tunis in February 1989, a month after he publicly renounced terrorism and agreed to a Palestinian state alongside Israel. He had convinced Wayne and me both that he was ready to make the compromises necessary for peace. Fragments of conversations from that meeting now came back to me.

We had been sitting around a large dinner table with Arafat and his colleagues in Tunis, and I was probing him, trying to understand his positions on the main issues surrounding a two-state solution to the Israeli-Palestinian conflict.

"Everything is to be put on the table," Arafat had assured me at that first meeting. "Borders, security, settlements, refugees, water, sources of water, corridors, labor forces."

Wayne had pressed him, "Everything is on the table?"

"Everything on the table," Arafat said. "They have to understand our fears, and we have to understand theirs."

Now, eleven years had passed, and Arafat was finally being given the opportunity he had told us he so earnestly wanted, to negotiate a final settlement with everything on the table. But instead of jumping at such an opportunity, he was not willing to compromise at all on many important issues. He had made it clear, for example, at Camp David and since, that he would not renounce the issue of the right of return. But that issue alone, and Arafat knew this, was enough to convince Israelis that any peace made with the Palestinians would lead to the end of Israel as a Jewish state. So if he continued to raise this issue, what did that mean about his ultimate intentions?

For years, when I had gone around telling people that I knew Arafat and that he wanted peace, I was often criticized as naïve, and as having been taken in by him. And I had always been sure that it was my critics, not me, who were wrong. But now, on this evening, the old questions swirled in my head. Did Arafat ever intend to make peace with Israel on terms that Israel could accept? Were the seven years of the Oslo peace process flawed from the very start?

Barak, too, had now pinned his entire career on the assumption that the Palestinians had negotiated in Oslo in good faith. And the irony was that Barak, unlike Rabin and Peres, had originally mistrusted the gradualist nature of the Oslo Accords, while accepting its core principle of ultimate partition of the land. It had been very difficult for Barak to act against his mentor, and he had told me of the furious argument he had had with Rabin at the time. Barak thought that it was a mistake to wait three years until beginning permanent status negotiations, because if those negotiations didn't work out, then Israel would have, in Barak's words, "given away assets," and received nothing in return. His attitude, therefore, was that Israel had to start with permanent status negotiations, and see if the other side was sincere and ready for peace.

Rabin, of course, thought it was Barak who was being unreasonable, since there was no readiness, certainly on Israel's side, to enter into permanent status discussions on the toughest issues at the very outset of the negotiating process. Rather, the three years were needed to build up trust, which, in the process, would pave the way for permanent status negotiations. Entering into permanent status negotiations at the outset, when the attitudes on both sides were still so mistrustful, would simply guarantee the failure of the talks.

Shimon Peres, the foreign minister at the time, and an architect of the Oslo Accords, had an even more fundamental objection to Barak's arguments. What Barak saw as the "giving away of assets," made no sense at all to Peres. In what way were the West Bank and Gaza, filled as they were with millions of resentful, militant Palestinians, assets? Rather, they were poison pills. By handing over these territories to the Palestinian Authority, Israel was, in effect, relieving itself of a terrible burden.

I remember what Peres had told me at the time: "You cannot run the life of another people. The problem is that Barak is a military person; if we are in control, he thinks that we dominate them." And Peres's feeling, which was mine as well, was that we were better off not dominating the Palestinians, but having nothing to do with running their lives.

But now, on this dark and pessimistic night, it seemed that Barak may have been right in insisting on going immediately to permanent status negotiations. Over these last years, Israel had handed territory over to the Palestinian Authority, in return for a promise of a cessation of violence. But the cessation of violence had not happened. Nor had the Palestinian Authority taken other actions that would have helped promote openness to peace and acceptance of Israel among the Palestinians. Rather, the textbooks used in the Palestinian schools continued to depict Israel and Jews in the most hateful terms.

But what to do now? Just give up on the talks and on the peace process? To me, it still seemed that a full-fledged collapse of negotiations would cause dire results. For one thing, the longer the stalemate continued, the greater the chance for renewed violence. Second, with Clinton's term as president about to expire, we were moving into the unknown. Clinton had invested himself in the Middle East far more than any other president. If he failed, there would be no incentive for a future president to invest efforts in what seemed to be a no-win situation.

And so, four nights later, on September 24, 2000, we went to meet Arafat again, this time in his Gaza compound, instead of in Ramallah. We took off that night from Tel Aviv in a helicopter. I remember looking out over the city's beach, lit up by the strip of hotels that line the coast of Tel Aviv to the edge of Jaffa's ancient port. Light always evokes a feeling of energy and excitement, even of joy. But it was hard to feel joyful that night.

We were met in Gaza by a Palestinian driver, who whisked us off straight to Arafat's compound, a large old villa on the beach. The truth is, Arafat lived extremely simply, in a small bedroom with a cot. I saw the bedroom once when he let me use the bathroom. The impression I had was that he lived like a wartime general. The office in which he received people was more spacious, and over his desk there was a big picture of the Dome of the Rock. He ate simply, and as well, healthfully, almost always including Arab lentil soup, into which he would put vegetables.

Anyway, it was 9:15 when we got there, and we sat down with Arafat, Abu Mazen, Saeb Erekat, and Nabil Abu Rudeineh around a large dining room table.

Despite the tensions of the recent weeks, the atmosphere was cordial. Over the many years of negotiations, a lot of affection had developed among these men, Wayne, and me.

Abu Mazen and Erekat started talking about the proposals—the "bridging proposals," as they were called—we could expect to hear from the administration in Washington. But the Palestinians were upset because the Americans seemed to be stalling their presentation. Erekat was complaining that he had been told *not* to request a meeting with the secretary of state. It later became clear that Albright did not want to invest herself in further negotiations during the current stalemate.

Of one thing, I felt certain. If there was going to be a break in the stalemate, it was not going to come because of actions taken by Madeleine Albright or even by the president. As I now said, pointing at Arafat: "The decisions have to be made by two people, you and Barak."

In characteristic manner, Arafat refused to accept responsibility. "I never make any decisions alone. I always discuss it—on every decision."

"That's the right way to do it," I said. I meant of course that it was right for him to talk to as many people as he wanted in advance. But when the time came to act, he would have to meet with Barak, and they would have to come to an agreement. "Rabin did the same," Arafat continued. "Netanyahu did the same. Shimon Peres did the same, large and small decisions. Begin made decisions alone. Barak is like Begin."

The thought occurred to me that, even if true (in point of fact, Begin had consulted extensively with Moshe Dayan and Ezer Weizmann, among others), Begin acting alone, if he did, had not exactly been a catastrophe. That's how a peace agreement with Egypt had been achieved.

I was prepared for the uncertainty, the stalling, and the indecision. But I also knew that I didn't want to leave that night without something tangible being achieved. "Tomorrow night, the prime minister would like to meet with you in his house in Kochav Yair, and he is inviting you to come to his home." Obviously, my words had been directed to Arafat, but it was Erekat who answered. "We would like to have the dinner in Ramallah, at Abu Mazen's home first. We will come to Barak's home for the second meeting. We are saying yes to tomorrow night." I knew it was important to Barak that they come to his home, but I was also very pleased; at least we had set up a meeting.

"At what time? When does Barak prefer to come?" Erekat now asked.

The Palestinians also expressed nervousness about the agenda. They felt they needed time to formulate their positions with greater certainty.

I did not want to run the risk of the meeting again being delayed. But I knew that there was one issue that would have to be addressed. I turned to Arafat: "I think Barak would prefer a quiet meeting just with you. You could all meet first, have a visit, but then a private meeting, just between you and Barak. Both of you want to make peace between each other so a tête à tête would be most appropriate in getting you to talk about how to break the impasse."

Erekat did not like the idea of Barak and Arafat meeting alone, possibly making decisions. For years, and most notably throughout the negotiations on permanent status, Erekat was always seated alongside Arafat, advising him every step of the way. I reiterated to Arafat, "The most important thing is to bring the two of you together, in a good atmosphere. It should be an opening for the other meetings. A rapprochement. But no agendas. We've had agendas before, but each side comes with maximalist positions."

I said now, "I'll call him."

Wayne and I left the dining room to call the prime minister in private. Wayne picked up the phone in the foyer, but we couldn't get an outside dial tone. We were struck by the absurdity of what was happening. Here we were, at the headquarters of Arafat and the PLO, trying to put through a call to Israel's prime minister, a call that could help bring peace between Israel and the Palestinians, and our efforts were being blocked because we couldn't get the telephone to work properly. Finally, we had to call in Abu Rudeineh, Arafat's assistant, to get an outside line.

We finally got through. "Arafat agrees to dinner," I told Barak, "but he wants it at Abu Mazen's home." I could see Arafat and the others standing in the doorway outside the room.

Barak replied, "It can't be there. I've been there three times already. It's only courteous for him to come to my home."

I said, "Come on, we're talking about war and peace here, let's forget about formalities."

But Barak would not let go. "It has to be in my home. Do me a favor. Go to Arafat and give him a hug for me and tell him, 'This is from Ehud, and he wants you to please accept the invitation and come to his home.'"

I put down the phone and returned to the dining room. I went over to Arafat, gave him a big hug, and said, "Abu Amar"—Arafat's *nom de guerre*—"this hug is from Ehud, and he says please meet him at his home. You're talking about making peace between Israel and the Palestinians, please do it."

"I don't know," Arafat responded.

"Just do me a favor. I never ask you for favors. Please come to his house for dinner. Do it for me."

Arafat looked right behind him, at his three aides. All three were shaking their head no, insisting that the meeting had to be at Abu Mazen's.

But I had spoken to Barak, and though I didn't fully understand the reasoning on both sides, I knew how important this issue was to him. "I know you want to host it," I told them, "but please accept this invitation. Please. It is very important. Please go along with him this time and get together."

Arafat looked me in the eye and said, "Okay. I'll go."

I went over to him and gave him a big hug, and said, "That's from me, and thank you very much."

Wayne later told me that he was wondering if they had rehearsed the whole scene, in other words, that the other three men had agreed in advance to shake their heads. That way, when Arafat finally agreed, it would be as a big favor.

Wayne might well have been right. There are many ways to wage diplomacy, and sophisticated planning and plotting is only one of them. Sometimes, a hug and friendship does the trick. That incident, which is still vivid in my mind, illustrated for me yet another aspect of Arafat's character. He was reluctant to act on requests if they were not asked in a personal way.

We left Arafat's compound at 10:45, and flew straight back to Barak's Jerusalem residence to brief him on the conversation. Although it was by now after midnight, Barak was fully alert and seemed quite pleased with what we told him. He even congratulated us, and I had not received many congratulations from Barak in the past. It was decided that the meeting would take place the next night, as we had discussed, at Barak's Kochav Yair home, a Tel Aviv suburb.

Late as it was, Wayne and I left Barak's residence and went out for a steak dinner. We felt we had the right to celebrate, me with a vodka and Wayne with a Coke. This meeting might well restart the process that had been painfully terminated two months earlier at Camp David. I was feeling pretty excited, and even put through a call to the White House to report to the president on what had happened. My call was in turn patched through to California where the president was playing golf. I gave him a brief report on our meetings, and he was pleased.

The next night, my driver picked me up at the Tel Aviv Hilton for the drive to Barak's house. En route, I remember the thoughts that went through my head: *This is an historic meeting. We could have a real breakthrough tonight. Barak pushed for the meeting so that means he wants to do something more than what he did at Camp David, or at the very least he wants to develop a better relationship with Arafat than he had there. So maybe it would be really important if President Clinton were to call Barak's home and encourage both of them to go forward and do their best to configure a peace.*

I called my secretary in Palm Beach and she put me through to Betty Currie, the president's secretary. I told her I needed to speak to the president. She got me through to him, and I said, "Mr. President, thanks for taking the call. I'm on my way to Barak's home. He and Arafat are going to have dinner and talk about moving the peace process forward. I think it would be incredibly important if you were to call Barak's home about an hour after Arafat gets there and encourage both of them to move forward. It would be a really strong message to both of them to get this thing done."

The president, who was onboard Air Force One, assured me, "Okay, I'll do it."

By the time I finished our phone call, the car was already pulling up outside the prime minister's home.

I was the first guest to arrive, and Barak looked very nervous. I remember him saying, "Where is Arafat going to sit? Where am I going to sit? Where is everyone else going to sit?" If the situation wasn't so serious, it would have been funny. He was adjusting and readjusting chairs in the living room. He pretty much ignored me, but again, I didn't take it personally. It was obvious how tense Barak was. I could only imagine that as he was walking around the room, rearranging the room, he must also have been rehearsing different strategies in his head. I later learned that his team had been advising him on the best approach to end the stalemate: Take Arafat aside shortly after he arrives, and tell him, "We've reached an impasse. We're at risk of letting a historical occasion slip by. Your team and our team are doing extraordinary, really creative work, and they're trying to reach an accord. But we leaders are the ones who are responsible for setting up the broad principles that can serve as the basis for the negotiations. The compromise on which the Americans are working is not in our interest. A negotiated settlement between us is preferable. We're at the moment of truth."

Barak was surrounded by his top advisors: Minister of Public Security Shlomo Ben-Ami, Minister of Transport Amnon Lipkin-Shahak, Senior Aide Danny Yatom, and, of course, Gilead Sher and Israel Hasson, the special aides to the negotiations.

Though the meeting itself had been kept secret, there were a handful of right-wing protestors across the street, pretty much permanently encamped there since the Camp David talks. The police had placed barricades at the street entrance to make sure the protestors didn't get any closer than they already were to the prime minister's residence. There also were guards with submachine guns and earpieces surrounding the house, and stationed at points along the street.

In a detail that now seems hard to believe, Arafat and his team were flown to the meeting on an Israeli military chopper.

Arafat and his team landed at a nearby helipad, and were driven to Barak's house. I think they managed to make it past the barricades without being recognized. When they pulled up to the house, Barak and his colleagues were standing outside to greet them. I remember that Arafat and Barak embraced, and Arafat even deposited a kiss on Barak's cheeks.

Nava Barak had prepared a generous spread of food, and brought out salads, bread, and large platters of Mideastern food, All the men there that night, despite the recent very deep tensions, knew each other well and talked freely.

Barak stood up, thanked me for arranging the meeting, and said that he believed peace could be achieved by the people gathered in this room. Even as he was speaking,

Gilead Sher and Saeb Erekat were whispering among themselves, trying to set an agenda for the evening. No one seemed to know exactly what topics should be discussed. Arafat followed Barak with a similar sort of vague, but positive, speech. But there remains to this day a very important difference of recollections regarding exactly what Arafat said. News had broken earlier that day that Sharon was planning to visit the Temple Mount (what the Muslims call Haram al Sharif), in order to demonstrate Israel's sovereignty over the holy site. Erekat insists that during his remarks, Arafat turned to Barak, and said, "Your Excellency, it is to no good end that Sharon will go to the Haram. Please don't allow him to go. Don't allow him to go because in a few months time, he will be the only one smiling. He will destroy us. Please don't give him permission to go." According to Erekat, Barak never responded to Arafat's request. The Israeli team claims they never heard such a request. But I do know that the issue of Sharon's visit was discussed. I remember Barak saying to me toward the end of the evening that Israeli law would not permit him to prevent the visit of a private Israeli citizen, which Sharon then was, to the Temple Mount.

After the two statements, I asked Barak and Arafat to discuss matters in a more private setting. I know that Erekat was unhappy with me pushing the two men to do so. He thought it was a bad idea to send them out alone, without any previously determined talking points. Erekat was not comfortable at the thought of what might happen in an extemporaneous meeting. My thinking, of course, was precisely the opposite. In my view, the well-planned overly thought-out meetings of the past few months were precisely what had gotten us into this predicament. Maybe a little spontaneous show of goodwill was precisely what could get us back on track.

The two men picked up a plate, filled it with food, and headed to Barak's outdoor patio table. We could see them through the glass sliding door. Barak put Arafat at the head of the table, and he sat on his left. The rest of us stayed inside eating and talking. To this day, we don't know exactly what was said, but it was clear that they were both talking in an animated way, and I had never seen them sitting so close and talking like two old friends.

Inside, the two peace teams were joking about the leaders on the porch, called them "the braves," a sort of gentle mockery of Arafat's by now overused cliché, "the peace of the brave." But there was nervousness in the laughter as well; the poor dynamic that had long existed between Arafat and Barak was known to everyone present, and it was hard to believe that it could be all overcome in a few minutes on Barak's patio. But I know what I was thinking: *Wow, this is great.*

And then the phone rang, and it was the president. They gave the phone to me, and I said, "Mr. President, hold on a second and I will get the prime minister and President Arafat." Abu Rudeineh went outside and brought the two leaders in. And I said, "Mr. President, here is Prime Minister Barak," and Barak said, "No, no, no, Arafat talks first." And Arafat said, "No, no, no. The prime minister talks first." And Barak said, "No, no, no. You have to talk first." They went back and forth, it was funny. The whole thing put everyone in mind of those early moments at Camp David when Barak and Arafat playfully tried to push each other through the door of the president's Maryland retreat. Finally, Arafat picked up the phone and talked to the president, and then Barak did.

Obviously, we could only hear one side of the conversation, but the two men assured Clinton that they would exhaust all options for an agreement, and that they had instructed their teams to do everything to bridge the gaps.

The meeting ended well after midnight. The feeling in the room was decidedly more upbeat than when we had arrived just a few hours earlier. Most important, the negotiating teams were now set to fly to Washington to continue the talks. Barak walked Arafat outside and took him privately in his car right to the helipad. Again, no one knows what was said, but it was clear that the two men were acting in a warm and friendly manner.

I left the meeting feeling more optimistic than I had in a good while, and very happy that we, Wayne and I, had helped bring the two men together. And when *Ma'ariv* and the *Jerusalem Post* interviewed the prime minister just a few days later, he spoke about the encounter very positively: "The meeting was very good, warm and open. We did not discuss the question of what percent of the territories will be in the settlement bloc, or how to handle the refugee problem, or what solution will be found for the matter of the Temple Mount, but we spoke of the necessary responsibility, the guarantees between us and the Palestinians, and of the need to solve a problem that is far more difficult than our problems with Jordan, Egypt, or even with Syria....The meeting was also open on a personal level, with memories shared. Arafat told us about his time in a Syrian prison, about his meetings with world leaders, that, in fact he knows them all. The [telephone] conversation with Clinton was especially moving and, of course, I tussled with Arafat, like at Camp David, over who would talk first. In the end, he spoke first, because he was the guest." When pressed about the chances for the two sides reaching an accord, Barak was straight down the middle, "Fifty-fifty," which might sound somewhat pessimistic, but which was certainly far more optimistic than he, or the Israeli public, would have felt about the possibilities of such an accord just one week earlier. As Barak emphasized, if such an accord were to come about, then this meeting had helped make it possible, "by creating a little more trust, and by contributing a little to the understanding between the sides that an arrangement will be reached not only by each side realizing its sense of justice, but rather that each will see with open eyes the motivation of the other."

My mood in fact would have remained very upbeat except for a meeting that took place on the day following the Barak-Arafat get-together. It was a meeting that puzzled me when it took place, and with the passage of time, it has come to puzzle me even more.

It all began the next day when Wayne and I went to the East Jerusalem neighborhood of Abu Dis to meet Abu Ala, the speaker of the Palestinian Legislative Council and a prime negotiator at Oslo. Abu Ala is a man I have long regarded with warmth and great respect. I always try to see him whenever I'm in Israel. I regard him as a good friend. At this meeting, we hoped to discuss Sharon's planned visit the following day to the Temple Mount, and I wanted to understand Abu Ala's take on the visit.

Whether or not Arafat raised this issue the preceding night, urging Barak to prohibit the visit, one did not have to be a prophet to realize that the visit had the potential to become violent, and spark riots.

We found Abu Ala in a low mood, what I can only describe as a sort of post-traumatic shock reaction to the breakdown of the Camp David talks. He had invested years of his life, and tremendous emotional energy, in trying to bring about a Palestinian state and coexistence with Israel—he was the Palestinian father of the Oslo Accords—and everything had seemed to crumble. Worse, he felt this whole catastrophe could have been avoided. He told us of a call he had received on July 3 at three in the morning. The caller was Hillary Clinton, and she told him that she and the president were vacationing on a boat, and Bill wanted to speak with him. When the president got on the line, he asked Abu Ala whether he should arrange a summit: Were the sides ready? Abu Ala told us that he strongly emphasized to the president that it was not a good idea, that the sides, certainly the Palestinian side, needed more time. But it was also clear to him from the tone, questions, and comments of the president that the decision had already been made.

Abu Ala then continued musing about the mistakes that had happened at Camp David, which had only worsened an already bad situation. I tried to bring him out of this topic, by turning to the current crisis that was now brewing, which I was convinced could be averted.

And so, knowing that within twenty-four hours Sharon would be arriving with a large Israeli police force at the Temple Mount, I said to Abu Ala: "Why don't you go up there, as head of the house, and greet Sharon. Tell him: 'Welcome to our home, to our holy place. Let me escort you, and show you around.' And have two guides there with you, archaeologists, who will show him around with you. Then, walk him back to the door, and say, 'Thank you very much for the visit.'" I kept pressing him; I remember I used an analogy from the world of martial arts: "When someone throws a punch, you get out of the way and grab his wrist, and pull him in the same direction as the punch, and he almost assuredly is going to go to the floor, because all his weight is in the punch." In other words, take what could be construed by Palestinians as an act of aggression by the Israelis, and by acting the role of a polite host, disarm Sharon. I wanted the Palestinians to feel that this was not a visit of aggression. What could Sharon do after such a polite and friendly reception? He certainly wouldn't respond with an aggressive and provocative statement.

Abu Ala acknowledged that there was merit to my suggestion. "That's a good idea," he said. My hopes soared, but then he added on the words that have puzzled me ever since. "I can't do it. It's too late."

What, in heaven's name, did that mean? No one ever knows exactly what someone else means, but I certainly was expecting a more positive response. So when he said, "I can't do it. It's too late," I was confused.

Too late for what?

In the years since (we've remained very friendly), I've asked Abu Ala several times what he meant by his comment, and I've never gotten an answer that satisfied me.

One further thought: Even though I now believe that the Second Intifada was a catastrophe waiting to happen, do I still think Barak erred in not stopping Sharon from making his visit? The answer is, it really is a moot question. For one thing, prior to the visit, Jibril Rajoub, the Palestinian West Bank security chief, had assured the Israelis that the Palestinian Authority would do everything it could to prevent an outbreak of violence. And once Barak received such an assurance, there was no way he would prohibit Sharon from making such a visit. He did warn Sharon that his act would be seen as provocative— not the sort of warning that, in any case, would have intimidated this general—but Barak felt he had no legal pretext for prohibiting such a visit. It is legal for every Israeli to visit the Temple Mount, so Barak felt his hands were tied.

Further, given that Barak was dovish, and perceived by Israelis as the most dovish prime minister in Israel's history, he feared, with reason, that if he prohibited Sharon's visit it would prove his weakness to the Israeli public, and thereby damage him politically, while strengthening the Israeli right wing. He could only imagine what the Israeli right would say: Now, with Barak in power, he does not even permit Jews, heroes like Sharon, to enter Israeli-held territory. Who knows what other concessions he is capable of making?

And so, with Barak assured that the Palestinians would contain any potential violence, Sharon went ahead and arrived that Thursday morning, September 28, 2000, at the Temple Mount. The visit was a brief one. The Palestinian demonstrators and onlookers, held back by Israeli security forces, watched as the group walked to the newly constructed exit of the Al-Aqsa Mosque, then turned around and left. There were some minor scuffles and rocks thrown, and nearly thirty people were lightly injured, the large majority of them Israeli police. I don't want to minimize what happened, but it was so minor in comparison to the rioting that erupted the next day that it really can be viewed as minor and almost insignificant.

It must be noted that Sharon, who has taken a lot of heat over this visit, conducted himself in a statesmanlike manner. After the short tour, he announced before TV cameras: *"I believe we can live together with the Palestinians. I came here to the holiest place of the Jewish people in order to see what happens here and to really have the feeling of how we need to move forward. There was no provocation here.*"

That same day, in Washington, at Dulles International Airport, Wayne met Mohammed Dahlan, the Gaza security chief and PLO negotiator. Dahlan was heading home from negotiations, while Wayne was flying back to Salt Lake City for a family event. Dahlan discussed with him, in an upbeat manner, the conversations that had been held, along with Ben-Ami, Sher, and Erekat, with Secretary of State Albright and Dennis Ross. According to Wayne, Dahlan was very animated, and seemed genuinely pleased. Most remarkably, he did not even mention Sharon's visit to the Temple Mount; the event did not seem to have registered on his radar screen.

The following day, a Friday and the Muslim day of prayer, many thousands of Palestinians, perhaps 20,000, thronged the Temple Mount for midday prayers at the three mosques there, Al-Aqsa, the Dome of the Rock, and Solomon's Stables. Cautioned that a demonstration might break out, Israeli riot police stationed themselves in the Western Wall Plaza, near the Lion's Gate.

At about 1:20 P.M., following the afternoon prayers, Palestinians at the Temple Mount began throwing stones at the Jews worshiping at the Western Wall. Yair Yitzhaki, the Jerusalem chief of police, immediately evacuated the worshippers from the Plaza, then was hit in the face by a stone and knocked unconscious. His face covered in blood, he was evacuated by ambulance to a hospital. His deputy, David Krauze, took control.

Krauze received information that the Palestinians were planning to storm the plaza at the Western Wall and the Jewish Quarter, and he organized his men, armed with riot gear and rifles, into formation along the ramp leading to the Mugrabi Gate, which separates the Temple Mount from the ramparts of the Western Wall. At about 1:30, the police charged onto the Temple Mount, and began firing rubber bullets at the crowd.

The clash between the police and the demonstrators lasted four hours. At one point, the police called Jibril Rajoub and asked him to persuade the demonstrators to stop throwing stones. At this stage, the police retreated to the adjacent Mugrabi Gate, and awaited developments. But the attempt, if made, failed.

Meanwhile, Palestinians throughout the West Bank and Gaza were watching the fighting on television, and many took to the streets to demonstrate. There is some reason to believe that these demonstrations and riots had been previously planned by the Palestinian Authority, and that the television and news coverage simply increased the size of the demonstrations. In any case, demonstrators started targeting Israeli army patrols and checkpoints and threw stones and Molotov cocktails. That same day, the Israeli army suspended all joint patrols with Palestinian police because a Palestinian officer shot dead an Israeli border guard near Qalqilya. By 5:30 P.M. 6 Palestinians were dead, and 200 injured, along with 14 injured Israeli police. By the next morning, the demonstrations were fully under the control of the Tanzim, young militants loyal to Arafat. They would disperse themselves among the thousands of demonstrators throughout the West Bank and Gaza, and provoke them to acts of violence. As Marwan Barghouti, their leader, declared on September 29, 2001, the first anniversary of the Intifada, "When Sharon visited the Al-Aqsa Mosque, this was the most appropriate opportunity for the outbreak of the Intifada."

As I watched the rioting on television, and saw the West Bank and Gaza go up in flames, along with the

peace process, it was hard to believe, and painful to recall, that just five days earlier I had watched Arafat and
Barak conversing convivially on Barak's patio. Among the
meetings these two men had held, this certainly had
been the finest and the warmest. Saeb Erekat had spoken of the "festive atmosphere, infused with a real sense
of happiness." And Barak had described the meeting to
the press as "moving," and recalled telling President
Clinton on the telephone, within earshot of Arafat: 'I'm
going to be the partner of this man even more than Rabin
was."

A week later, on October 4, Barak and Arafat met
again, this time in the residence of the U.S. ambassador
to Paris; at the time, the United States was doing what it
could to engineer a cease-fire. When Barak asked Arafat
to reign in Barghouti, the PLO leader feigned ignorance.
"Who?" he asked. "Who?" Barak repeated the name with
a strong Arabic inflection, and Arafat again said, "Who?
Who?" The historian Benny Morris reports that, at this
point, Arafat's aides, amused by the way their chief was
playing with the increasingly frustrated Barak, couldn't
keep themselves from laughing. Arafat finally stopped
pretending that he didn't know who Barghouti was, and
agreed to call him later.

Was the dinner at Kochav Yair, therefore, just a fantasy,
a pleasant but ultimately meaningless interlude? That is
how the hardliners on both sides choose to view it, either
as a set-up by the Palestinians at worst, or as a last gasp of
peace before the outbreak of violence at best. I see it
though as a small success that will someday be regarded
as more significant than the violence that followed it.
That violence has been and always will be an endless
cycle, the firing of bullets and the setting off of bombs.
And each side goes on justifying its acts by pointing to

the even greater evil committed by the other side. All the cycle of violence ever leads to is grieving mothers and fathers, and two nations and peoples with obscenely high rates of wounded, crippled, and paralyzed people.

That's why my mind goes back, often, to that dinner at the prime minister's home. Successes like that, amid the tidal waves of despair, are the buoys of hope we hold onto to keep us afloat.

EIGHT

Are the 1967 Borders
Good for Israel?

After traveling the region for fifteen years, I have come to understand that the Arab/Israel conflict comes down to borders—to secure, recognized, and permanent borders that can only come from agreements with Israel and its Arab neighbors. Today, Israel is a state without borders, and Palestine is not yet a state. It seems to me that, at the end of the day, Israel will somehow agree with the Palestinians, all the Arab states, and the Americans that the 1967 borders with modifications and land swaps will, in fact, be the secure, recognized, and permanent borders of the State of Israel.* On that day, Israel and its Arab neighbors will come to an end of their

---

* While the territorial issue is critical, resolution must also be found to the refugee issue and finessing sovereignty to the holy sites in and around Jerusalem's walled city, that would take into account the historical attachment and reverence of all religions and people.

interminable, often armed conflict. And on that day, Israel, her people, the Arab world, and the entire world will be a better place.

Admittedly, this will not be an easy accomplishment. Decades ago, after the 1967 War, Israel asked many of its citizens to form defensive settlements in the West Bank and Gaza, to build homes, schools, synagogues, industries, and farms there, and to build a life for themselves in what they hoped would be a return to the biblical land of Israel.

These people are heroes, and now the State of Israel will be asking these families to give up their homes there, and develop homes and lives for themselves within what will become the new permanent borders of Israel. Not an easy request to make of anyone. But I am sure that when they understand that this is for the greater good of Israel, and that there is no alternative, they will in fact pull up their roots once again and return to the new recognized and secure borders of Israel.

At the same time, there must be an impenetrable security fence all along the new and recognized border dividing the two states, which will enable Israel to keep terrorists from infiltrating. And Israel must remain militarily stronger than all the Arab nations around her as a deterrent against any attack (a promise made by several American presidents, and which is now a part of American foreign policy).

Studies conducted by the Center for Middle East Peace and Economic Cooperation have repeatedly documented that between 75 and 80 percent of Israelis understand that the conflict between Israel and the Palestinians will be ended on these terms. As they well realize, holding onto the West Bank and its almost two million Palestinians is a danger to Israel that grows not only from year to year but from week to week.

But what if Israel withdraws from the West Bank and the Palestinians and Arab world don't keep the peace? Would withdrawal then have been a fateful, perhaps catastrophic, error? Not at all.

Even in this worst-case scenario, Israel is far stronger and safer without the West Bank and Gaza than with it. The West Bank and Gaza do not provide Israel with a safety net, a buffer zone if you will, but actually bring great danger into Israel's midst.

As has long been apparent to everyone familiar with the situation, the Palestinians do not want to be occupied. Who does? Jews should know from their own history how much people resent being ruled over by others. During much of the British occupation of Palestine between 1918 and 1948, the British did not go out of their way to mistreat the Jews. They permitted a more or less free press, the development of Hebrew language schools, and even a sort of shadow government formed by the Jewish Agency.

But ultimately, it was what the British did not permit that rankled and antagonized the Jews far more than what they did. Thus, for example, the British placed great restrictions on Jewish immigration into Palestine, a restriction that eventually cost the lives of hundreds of thousands, maybe millions, of Jews who wished to flee the Nazis.

Even more fundamentally, the British did not allow the Jews to create a state. Their refusal to do so eventually prompted the formation of two Jewish terrorist groups: the Irgun, headed by future prime minister Menachem Begin; and Lehi (Freedom Fighters of Israel), one of whose three leaders, Yitzhak Shamir, later also became a prime minister.

The British struck back at Jewish terror and hanged members of the Irgun and of Lehi. Not only did this not stop the terror, it provoked ever greater anti-British animosity among large segments of the Jewish population in Palestine. In those days, it was common to hear Jews compare the British to the Nazis, an accusation that hurt and inflamed the British (who had just spent six years fighting the Nazis)—as similar accusations hurt and inflame Israelis today.

Then, in 1948, England left Palestine and a Jewish state was declared.

Were many Israeli Jews still furious at the British even after they left? Of course. But once the British were gone (and this is the crucial point), the anger and animosity declined. By 1956, only eight years later, England was allied with Israel and France in the Suez War against Egypt.

Israel's presence in the West Bank is an ongoing provocation. It is hard to imagine that resistance against Israel, and support for terrorist acts against her, will cease before Israel gets out of almost all of the West Bank in an agreement with the Palestinians.

Once Israel does, its future will quickly become much brighter. Crown Prince (and now King) Abdullah of Saudi Arabia has repeatedly made it clear that Israel's withdrawal to the borders of 1967 will end the Arab conflict with Israel, and lead to normalization in relations with the Arab world. It will also ease relations with Europe as well. Within a few years of Israel's withdrawal and the creation of a Palestinian state, Israel will likely have diplomatic relations with fifteen or more Arab states, a position ratified in 2002 in a declaration at a meeting of the Arab League in Beirut.

The alternatives to the position outlined here are glum, and getting glummer. There are at least five pernicious effects the ongoing occupation of the West Bank has on Israel.

HUMAN SUFFERING

Israel can't hold on to the occupation of the West Bank without suffering the continuing death of many of its citizens.

Almost a thousand Israelis have died in the four years of the Second Intifada. That's an average of almost one Israeli life lost per day. And while erecting an impenetrable security fence around Israel is indispensable to guaranteeing Israelis greater security, it is equally important to end an occupation of a people that do not want to be occupied.

But terrorists infiltrating Israel is only one reason Israelis are dying. As long as Israel has troops—comprised largely of young men eighteen to twenty-one years old—stationed in the West Bank manning roadblocks and patrolling, then every year many of these soldiers will live in danger.

ECONOMIC COSTS

Maintaining the occupation is choking Israel. Over $60 billion have been spent over these last thirty-five years developing and protecting settlements on the West Bank, a diversion of funds that has several times sent Israel on an extended, downward economic stagnation and spiral.

Dov Zakheim, the former American undersecretary of defense and himself a committed Jew, said on a recent visit to Israel: *"You're taking money out of education, money out of welfare, money out of jobs, money out of infrastructure, and pouring it into the West Bank. Israel's society is suffering a lot as a result of the settlements."*

The diversion of such enormous amounts of money to develop and protect settlements in the West Bank has hurt Israel economically, especially on the domestic front. As of the fall of 2004, 20,000 municipal employees had not been paid in months, while Finance Minister Benjamin Netanyahu was trying to combat this situation by, among other things, lowering welfare payments to people who are already in terrible need.

Would all this change if Israel got out of the West Bank?

Definitely. Many billions of dollars would be freed up. Until then, money that is desperately needed inside Israel's 1967 borders for the underprivileged, for job expansion, and for the development of Israel's future in its south, in the Negev, and in the north in the Galilee, is used instead to subsidize the settlements.*

AT STAKE IS ISRAEL'S JEWISH IDENTITY AND DEMOCRACY

On October 25, 2004, Prime Minister Ariel Sharon, speaking before the Israeli Knesset, stated one of the most important reasons Israel must get out of Gaza: *"We do not wish to control millions of Palestinians who double in number in each generation. A democratic Israel will not be able to withstand such a thing."*

---

* Yet another blow to the economy derives from the decline in tourism, attributable in large part to a fear of visiting Israel; who would choose to spend their vacation in a country that has suicide bombings? (In recent months, the security fence has helped bring about a great decline in such attacks and a great rise in tourism. And now, in 2005, there is a cease-fire.) I have visited Israel an average of four or more times a year for the last fifteen years. But most potential tourists do not want to go with their families into a country they regard as a war zone.

Sharon, of course, limited his analysis to the threat posed to Israel's democracy by retaining Gaza. But the truth is, the threat emanating from holding on to the West Bank is even greater. There are more Palestinians on the West Bank—almost two million—than in Gaza, and they too are increasing in numbers far more rapidly than are Israeli Jews. For years, demographers have predicted that as early as 2010, the Arab population living within Israel, Gaza, and the West Bank will surpass in numbers the Jewish population. Recent studies suggest that equality in Jewish and Arab numbers might already exist. This means that Israel is now poised to cease being a Jewish state (its raison d'etre for existence) or a democratic one (the main reason Israel is the recipient of so much support in the United States). Ridding itself of Gaza, while holding on to the West Bank, will postpone the demographic finale of Israel as a Jewish state for some time, but not forever. And within the coming decades the problem will just get worse. Demographers now estimate that if the current trends continue, by 2050 Jews will make up roughly a third of the area's population.

With few exceptions, Jews both in Israel and throughout the world desire that Israel always retain two characteristics: its status as a Jewish state, and its democracy. Jews want a Jewish state for many reasons, one of them being that they are painfully aware of what can happen to Jews when they don't have a homeland. As Chaim Weizmann famously declared in the years after Hitler's rise to power: "There are now two sorts of countries in the world, those that want to expel the Jews and those that don't want to admit them." That is why the first law passed by the Knesset after Israel became a state was the Law of Return, guaranteeing any Jew anywhere in the world the right to come to Israel and to immediately become a citizen.

And Jews want Israel to be a democracy. Human dignity demands that every person is entitled to freedom. What else could be the meaning of the Torah's ancient teaching that every human being—Gentile no less than Jew, Arab no less than Israeli—is created in the image of God.

Unfortunately, as long as Israel holds on to the West Bank, it can't have both.

In the aftermath of the 1967 War, it was possible to avoid grappling with this issue. At that time, the Jews greatly outnumbered the Arabs and, in any case, most Israelis assumed that sooner or later there would be a settlement with Jordan, and the West Bank would be returned to Jordanian control. But those days are long past. Now, there remains only one way for Israel to retain both its character as a Jewish state and as a democracy, and that is to withdraw from parts of the West Bank and Gaza. These two areas have become "poison pills" for Israel. Either they will kill off the Jewishness of the state, or they will turn Israel into an apartheid society like that of the late and unlamented South Africa. Both are prices that few Jews are willing to pay.

IMMIGRATION TO ISRAEL

The effect of the Intifada on immigration to Israel is felt and likely to grow worse. In 2003, more Russian Jews chose to live in Germany than in Israel. If Jews are choosing to live in Germany over Israel, can you imagine how great the fear to live in Israel and the disinterest (because of the periodically declining economic situation) have become?

Some years ago, Benny Elon, a member of the Knesset and a former member of the Israeli Cabinet representing the Moledet Party, which advocates annexing the West Bank, used to argue that Israel had no long-term reason to fear the Arabs becoming a majority within Israel. American Jews, Elon insisted, would one day immigrate in vast numbers and solve the demographic problem once and for all.

For the Israeli right to base assumptions on Israel's future Jewish character on a migration of two or three million American Jews is, of course, unrealistic. Furthermore, even the immigration of one million Jews from the former Soviet Union in the 1990s did not reverse the Jewish demographic decline.

Yet, without an enormous migration of Jews to Israel, the Arabs will become the majority of Israel's population. This point cannot be overemphasized. If Israel holds on to the West Bank and Gaza, there is no alternative to Palestinians becoming the majority of Israel's population.

EMIGRATION

In the year 2003, 27,000 Israelis left Israel to live elsewhere. In the 1960s, during an economic downturn, a much smaller number of Israeli *yordim* (emigrants) prompted a famous cartoon in Israel, with the caption "Will the last person to leave Lod airport please turn off the lights?"

What has triggered an emigration of such massive numbers? More than anything, it is despair over terror, hopelessness over the situation in the territories, despondency over the weak economy, a general sense of gloom over Israel's future, and the prospect of a much happier, successful life elsewhere. It is impossible to imagine a happy future for Israel as long as it is mired in the occupation of the West Bank.

To the question, "How can Israel give up the West Bank and return the more than 60,000 Israelis living there back to Israel?" I counter, "How can Israel continue to hold onto the West Bank and permit a situation that is causing it to lose tens of thousands of Israelis a year to emigration?"

And to the question, "Will the return to the 1967 borders put Israel at risk?" I can only say that the 1967 borders are a blessing in comparison to the borders Israel now has. I know that to many these words sound jarring, but I assure you, they are true.

THE 1967 BORDERS: THERE IS NO OTHER REALISTIC ALTERNATIVE

I am a strong optimist. I firmly believe that one day there will be peace between Israel and her neighbors. Israel will return to the borders of '67 with modifications and land swaps and her neighbor will be an independent demilitarized democratic Palestinian state. And the United States will be a true partner and guarantor of that peace.

I know from decades of experience in business that if you want to keep your business thriving, you have to make sure that your employees, your suppliers, and your customers are satisfied and content. If they aren't, they will resent you, and unresolved resentment turns to animosity. In the case of business, your good employees quit, your suppliers stop dealing with you, and your customers shift to other products. In the case of countries, when one side is left feeling resentful peace will not last.

So Israel has a vested interest in making sure that in any final agreement, the Palestinians feel whole. Otherwise, there will not be an agreement.

In return for what they are giving up, the Israelis, no

less than the Palestinians, must feel whole as well. They must feel that Palestinians will accept once and for all—and without any qualifications—Israel's right to exist as an independent sovereign Jewish state. And, because of the long history of obsessive anti-Israel hatred in the Arab world, Israel, in order for it to feel secure, must continue now, and for the foreseeable future, to be stronger militarily than all the surrounding Arab countries, and in alliance with America.

A full 78 percent of Israelis are willing to accept two states for two people, as long as the Palestinian state is demilitarized, and the Palestinian refugees are settled in the new State of Palestine or other willing host countries, and not in Israel. They are willing to accept that Palestine's borders will be the 1967 borders with modifications. In other words, Israel will incorporate the largest West Bank settlements (which comprise less than 5 percent of the land) and, in return, will swap land from other parts of Israel, so that the Palestinians will end up with 100 percent of the land mass lost in 1967. And they are willing to accept that Jerusalem will be divided by population.*

Eighty-one percent of Israeli Arabs support such an agreement as well.

But will these wide-ranging concessions by Israel satisfy the appetite of the Palestinians? Will the West Bank Arabs support such an agreement? Some won't, just as

---

* These statistics reflect the responses given to polls conducted by the Center for Middle East Peace. Other polls have indicated somewhat lower support for a Palestinian state, but still a substantial majority. Thus, a January 2005 poll by the Palestinian Center for Policy and Survey Research, in cooperation with Hebrew University of Jerusalem, found that 70 percent of Israelis would be willing to accept a Palestinian state.

about 20 percent of Israelis would reject such an agreement, and would regard the status quo as preferable. But such Palestinians (and Israelis, too) are a minority, though unfortunately, a particularly vocal and militant minority. But a minority nevertheless.

What the majority of Palestinians want is an end to the occupation, and an end to the conflict. Many even want good relations with the State of Israel. They too have suffered enough, and they are ready for an end to this horrible conflict.

There are those—usually, but not always, on the Israeli right—who say that the Palestinians don't want peace, that Israel offered everything at Camp David, and that the Palestinian leadership turned it down.

But just because opportunities were missed in the past does not mean that we can give up on our quest for peace and an end to the conflict.

When I was a young salesman, the conventional wisdom was that the best sales are made after the fifth visit. So we must try and try again—and we will succeed. But we must do so with a sense of realism, and with offers that will make each side feel whole.

I recall a dinner I had with then Jerusalem mayor Ehud Olmert at the King David Hotel, which overlooks the walls of the Old City. I asked him if he would be willing to give up his life for these walls. He told me, "Yes." And I then asked him if he would be willing to sacrifice his son's life for these walls. He immediately said, "No. I would not."

But that's exactly what we're doing, and that's why we need to end this conflict. The Israeli novelist and essayist Amos Oz has put it eloquently: *"Every Israeli and every Palestinian knows that this land will be divided into two sovereign nations....One day when the peace treaty is achieved, and the Palestinian ambassador presents his credentials to the president of Israel in the Western section of Jerusalem, while the Israeli ambassador presents his credentials to the Palestinian president in East Jerusalem, we shall all have to laugh at the stupidities of our past. Even as we laugh, we shall have to answer for the spilling of so much innocent blood. But the mothers and fathers of the dead will not be laughing.*"

At the end of the day, peace will come when Israel and the Palestinians make the concessions and compromises that have been described throughout this book. I have based my assessment on over a thousand meetings with both Israeli and Arab leaders, and with U.S. diplomats and officials as well. I think back to the words of Crown Prince (now King) Abdullah of Saudi Arabia, approved by so many other Arab leaders, that if Israel will go back to the 1967 borders, then the Arab states will end the state of war with her and establish diplomatic relations. No one who has significant knowledge of the region believes that peace will come on any other terms.*

If we accept reality now, then peace can come now, and fewer people will die. If Hillel defined the essence of Judaism as "What is hateful unto you, don't do unto your neighbor. The rest is commentary," I would say that the essence of the solution to the Israeli/Palestinian conflict, and the Israeli-Syrian one as well, is "Negotiate the

---

* However, the Arab states need to be far more publicly explicit in telling the Palestinians the truth that the refugees must go to Palestine and not Israel. Without this Arab compromise, there will not be peace. This is as important as the territorial issues in order to preserve the Jewish character of Israel, so compromises must be made by both sides.

peace along the 1967 borders with modifications, build a strong security fence, and maintain the best army in the region. The rest is commentary."

And what happens if we give in to reality? Good things. Not only will there be an end to fighting in the region (as has been the case with the cold peace with Egypt, and the somewhat warmer peace with Jordan), but Israel will finally be able to turn its attention inside, to itself, to the Negev, for example. It is the Negev and the Galilee, not the West Bank, that are Israel's future, and I can say with confidence that five years after the occupation ends, we will have greened the Negev with desalinated water. The Negev makes up more than half of Israel's land mass, but it has been ignored, and will remain ignored as long as Israel retains the West Bank.

Near the end of the Torah, the Bible cites God's words to the Jewish people: "I have set before you life and death. Choose life that you may live" (Deuteronomy 30:19). If we want to choose life for ourselves, and even more for our children, let us do now what we are going to have to do, in any case, at the end of the day.

Let us choose life and let us choose peace. At least thirty times a day in the prayer book, we pray for peace. We hear God's promise: "God will give strength to his people, God will bless His people with peace."

For most of our history, the Jewish people had neither strength nor peace. A large part of the dream of Zionism has been fulfilled. Jews have been blessed with strength—the first Jews in over two thousand years to have such power—so that Jews, not their enemies, can make the political decisions that will shape the Jewish people's future.

Now we have to choose the blessing of peace as well.

Herzl's visionary words remain truthful and right: "If we will it, it is no dream."

Adonai oz le'amo ye-teyn. "God will give strength to His people. God will bless his people with peace."

God has given His people strength. The blessing of peace is now in our hands to fulfill.

July 2005: As Israel Prepares to Leave Gaza

Having devoted so many years of effort in a bid to re-solve this conflict and having witnessed the horrific four and a half years of terror and violence beginning in 2000, I hope Israelis and Palestinians are beginning to emerge from their long tunnel. There are encouraging signs of courageous and farsighted leadership on both sides.

On the Israeli side, Prime Minister Ariel Sharon, pa-tron of the settlement movement, will be the one who will shatter the taboo and evacuate 8500 Israeli settlers from Gaza. This is a move of immense significance for two reasons. First of all, it will mark the first time since the 1967 war that Jewish settlers will be evacuated from areas that are likely to be a Palestinian state.* Shattering

---

* Sharon evacuated a quarter of that number from the Sinai as part of the 1979 peace treaty with Egypt, but that land was being returned to Egypt, and not being used to form a Palestin-ian state; in addition, the area of Sinai (though it did of course include Mount Sinai) did not have the same biblical resonance as did Gaza, which is mentioned in the biblical books of Joshua and Judges as part of Israel's biblical patrimony.

this taboo is likely to facilitate rather than impede further withdrawals, since the precedent will have been set. Therefore, it is no accident that some of the most vociferous opponents to Gaza withdrawal are West Bank settlers, who fear that they will be next. Second, it is critical that it is Sharon who is making this move. Yes, cynics will say that Sharon can pull it off since there will be no Sharon in the opposition to block it. Some will say it is historic justice, namely that the architect of the settlement movement is the one who is uniquely positioned to tell Israelis the truth about the future. Sharon is taking a bold move at great personal risk. The head of the Shin Bet, Israel's security service, has cautioned that there are 200 Israeli Jews who want to assassinate him. Yet, Sharon realizes that Israel's demographic future hangs in the balance.

As of this writing, it is hard to know the outcome of the Gaza withdrawal. There is no doubt that if the disengagement succeeds, and is followed by a continued decline in anti-Israel terrorism, that moderates on both sides will be emboldened to return to peacemaking. Alternatively, if it proves to be a fiasco, it will only serve the agendas of the extremists. I hope we look back at this summer as the beginning of the relaunching of a historic process.

Another sign of leadership is coming from the Palestinians. I knew Yasser Arafat for many years. Many Palestinians loved him for being the galvanizing force of Palestinians' national identity, while many Israelis, especially after the Intifada began in 2000, reviled him as a terrorist who ultimately could not become a statesman. I have my own views of this, but I prefer to focus on the future and not the past. Whatever one's view of Arafat, there is no doubt that his successor Abu Mazen (Mahmoud Abbas) has set a different tone. He ran a campaign in January 2005 on an explicit peace platform, making clear that violence is politically counterproductive. Violence is not making the reality of a Palestinian state closer, but rather more distant. Therefore, it is not coincidental that support for the current cease-fire is high and support for suicide bombings against Israel has dropped by 48 points in the polls since Arafat's death. This is an opportunity that provides a better climate for future peacemaking. Of course there are still challenges. But one thing is clear. Rejectionists should not be allowed to break the cease-fire and return to the ways of 2000–2004. The trust between the parties was shattered during those years, and rebuilding the trust will not be easy. Violence is the surest way to ensure that the trust will never be regained.

That is why there is no alternative but to continue to try to make the inroads that will one day lead to peace. And so the meetings continue, a get-together with my friend of thirty years, Prime Minister Arik Sharon in late May 2005, and a breakfast meeting organized with American Jewish leaders in Washington, D.C., for Palestinian president Abu Mazen.

In recent polls conducted by the most respected pollsters, 68 percent of the Palestinian people in the West Bank and Gaza said that when they vote for president the most important thing they want is an end to corruption. The second most important thing is that the leader bring them to peace with Israel. Likewise, a recent poll in Israel also showed that 78 percent of the Israelis want to see peace and an end of the conflict with the Palestinians. And all of those people are ready to sacrifice and compromise in order to reach this peace. The majority of people on both sides want peace. Now is the perfect time for the leaders of the United States, Israel, and Palestine to get together and forge the peace that the people so desperately want.

As the Torah declares: "I have set before you life and death, the blessing and the curse. Therefore, choose life." And in today's world, that means choose peace.

ACKNOWLEDGMENTS

All my efforts to help bring peace to the Middle East started with my friendship with Wayne Owens. Very quickly, Wayne became my partner and mentor in an attempt to bring about reconciliation between Israel and her neighbors. A man of boundless optimism, energy, and good will, it is an honor for me to dedicate this book to his memory.

It is also a particular honor for me that former President Bill Clinton has written the Foreword for this book. I have long been very grateful for President Clinton's friendship and guidance. I am also pleased to express my gratitude to other members of his administration who helped me in the carrying out of my efforts at private diplomacy, among them former Secretary of State Madeleine Albright and former National Security Advisor Sandy Berger.

In Israel, I have been blessed with the friendship of

Prime Minister Ariel Sharon, former Prime Minister Shimon and Sonia Peres, Vice Prime Minister Ehud and Aliza Olmert, and the late President Chaim Herzog (Vivian), his wife Aura, and Boojie Herzog, their son and my long-time legal adviser, friend, and confidante.

In the Arab world, I was treated consistently with the greatest kindness and courtesy by the late King Hassan II of Morocco and his adviser Andre Azoulai, the late King Hussein of Jordan and his son King Abdullah, Egyptian President Hosni Mubarak and his senior advisor Dr. Osama El-Baz, the late Syrian president Hafez Assad, the late Palestinian president Yasser Arafat, President Abu Mazen, Prime Minister Abu Ala, chief negotiator Saeb Erekat, and Sari Nusseibeh, the president of Al-Quds University.

In Washington, I want to thank the members of the Center for Middle East Peace and Economic Cooperation, whose loyalty and dedication was and remains indispensable in carrying out the mission Wayne and I undertook in 1988: Avi Gil, Toni Verstandig, Dan Rothem, Gigi Ghanim, my indispensable adviser Sarah Ehrman, Jim Gerstein, Sahana Dharmpri, and Professor Stephen P. Cohen who, over several years, shared with us his expertise in conflict resolution.

I would like to thank Joseph Telushkin who worked carefully with me to turn my fifteen years of experiences into narrative form, and to Dan Grushkin for his extensive research and early rendering of this material. My personal staff was equally crucial in bringing this book to fruition: Charles Noonan, Paul Austin, Brad Bleefeld, Darlene Rowley, and Karen Shumilla. Josh Lookstein, the energetic and creative head of the Dan Abraham Foundation, played a crucial role in shepherding this book through the entire process. Bonny Fetterman, who joined us late in the process, played an integral role as agent in connecting us with our publisher and in helping bring about the book's publication in a timely manner. And I would like to thank Nili Doft for her typing and transcribing.

I would also like to thank Dr. George Blackburn of Harvard Medical School who, as my closest friend, has nurtured and mentored me both physically and intellectually.

Acharon acharon chaviv, last and most beloved, I wish to thank my wife Ewa, and my children Rebecca, Leah, Tammy, Simmy, Sarah, and Sam, my sons-in-law, and my twenty-one beautiful grandchildren. I thank them for all their love and support and the sacrifices they have made to enable me to follow my dreams. And also my brother, Jerry, and my sister, Judy, and my brother-in-law and dear friend Dr. Eddie Steinberg whose love and friendship have been among the greatest blessings in my life.

Any profits that accrue from this book are being donated to Seeds of Peace, an organization devoted to bringing Israeli, Palestinian, and other children from Arab lands together for a summer camp experience, at which they can learn about and from each other, and who will most enjoy the blessing of peace.

Key Figures

PRINCE ABDULLAH—The de facto leader of Saudi Arabia after King Fahd's disabling 1995 stroke, and King since Fahd's death in 2005.

ABU ALA (Ahmed Qurei)—Currently the prime minister of the Palestinian Authority and a longtime Palestinian leader. He was one of the primary figures responsible for the Oslo agreement.

ABU MAZEN (Mahmoud Abbas)—Currently the president of the Palestinian Authority and the head of the PLO. Served for many years as Arafat's number-two man, and was one of the primary figures responsible for the peace process.

NABIL ABU RUDEINEH—Arafat's longtime chief of staff, and one of his closest aides. Currently runs the president's office.

FARUK AL-SHARA—Syria's foreign minister. Led the failed negotiations for Israeli-Syrian agreement in 1999–2000.

YASSER ARAFAT—The late Palestinian leader, and by far the most significant figure in the movement of Palestinian nationalism. Served as head of the PLO, the PA, and Fatah until his death on November 11, 2004.

HASSAN ASFOUR—Close aide to Arafat and a Palestinian negotiator.

HAFEZ ASSAD—the late Ba'athist Syrian president who ruled over Syria from 1970 until his death in 2000.

EHUD BARAK—Currently member of the Labor Party. Former Israeli prime minister (1999–2001), foreign minister, defense minister, and IDF chief of staff. Barak is best known for his negotiations with Arafat at Camp David (2000), under the aegis of President Clinton.

OSAMA EL-BAZ—Senior advisor to Egyptian President Hosni Mubarak.

WILLIAM JEFFERSON "BILL" CLINTON—U.S. president (1993–2001), hosted Mideast peace summit between Barak and Arafat at Camp David in the summer of 2000.

MOHAMMAD DAHLAN—Currently the PA minister of civil affairs. Longtime leader of the PA Preventive Security forces in Gaza and a Palestinian negotiator.

SAEB EREKAT—A member of the Palestinian leadership. Has held various positions, most of which dealt with negotiations with Israel and media outreach.

MALCOLM HOENLEIN—Longtime executive vice-chairman of the Conference of Presidents of Major Jewish Organizations, and one of the most influential figures in American Jewish life.

KING HUSSEIN—Ruler of Jordan for almost fifty years until his death in 1999. King Hussein was a firm supporter of the peace process and signed a treaty with Israel in 1994.

WALID MOUALEM—Formerly the Syrian ambassador to the United States. He was the main counterpart of Itamar Rabinovich in the negotiations that took place during the Rabin area.

HOSNI MUBARAK—President of Egypt since the assassination of Anwar Sadat in 1981.

BENJAMIN NETANYAHU—Currently a member of Knesset and Israel's minister of finance. Former Israeli prime minister (1996-1999), foreign minister, ambassador to the UN, and a prominent Likud leader.

EHUD OLMERT—Currently a member of Knesset and Israel's vice prime minister and minister of industry, trade, and labor, and former mayor of Jerusalem. Long-time Sharon confidant and Likud activist.

WAYNE OWENS—the late congressman (D-Utah), president of the Center for Middle East Peace & Economic Cooperation, and Dan's closest friend and partner in the search for Israeli-Palestinian peace. He died of a heart attack in Tel Aviv in 2002 while on his ongoing mission to facilitate peace in the Middle East.

SHIMON PERES—Currently a member of Knesset (Labor) and Israel's vice premier and formerly Israel's prime minister (1984–1986), foreign minister, and minister of finance.

YITZHAK RABIN—Late prime minister of Israel (1974–1977 and 1992 until his assassination by an Israeli-Jewish extremist on November 4, 1995) and a member of Knesset. Formerly Israel's minister of defense and IDF chief of staff during the Six-Day War of 1967.

DENNIS ROSS—Chief U.S. envoy to the peace process. Headed the U.S. negotiation teams between 1991 and 2001.

YITZHAK SHAMIR—Former Israeli prime minister (1983–1984 and 1998–1992) and longtime Likud activist.

ARIEL SHARON—Current prime minister of Israel (since 2001) and a member of Knesset. Longtime Likud leader and a force in Israel's settlement enterprise.

Wayne Owens
1937–2002

In January 1993, after representing Utah in Congress for a total of eight years, Wayne Owens, Dan Abraham's partner in pursuit of a peace agreement between Israel and her neighbors, became the vice chairman of the Center for Middle East Peace and Economic Development. In February 1995, he became the Center's president. Earlier, while in Congress, Mr. Owens, a member of the Foreign Affairs Committee, chose to concentrate his committee efforts on the Middle East. He visited the region nearly every three months over the last five years of his service in Congress, usually accompanied by Mr. Abraham. In 1989, the two men organized the Center in order to support and promote the peace process, and to help build economic interaction between Israel and its Arab and Palestinian neighbors.

Traveling together, Mr. Owens and Mr. Abraham established a working relationship with nearly all the leaders of the region, relationships that have been described throughout this book. In addition, as the Center's president, Mr. Owens became renowned internationally as an honest peacemaker, known for his foresight in taking unprecedented steps toward mediation between Arab states and Israel.

Mr. Owens, the son of a sheepherder and a farmer, was born in Panguitch, Utah. He was a graduate of the

University of Utah college and law school. Prior to his service in Congress, Mr. Owens worked on the staffs of three United States senators: Frank Moss of Utah, Robert Kennedy of New York, and Edward Kennedy of Massachusetts. He practiced law in Utah and Washington, D.C., and was a member of the Utah State and United States Supreme Court bars.

Mr. Owens also devoted six years of his life to full-time service for the Church of Jesus Christ of Latter-Day Saints (Mormons). In 1980, he was appointed by President Jimmy Carter to the National Commission on Resource Conservation and in 1994 by President Bill Clinton to the Utah Reclamation Mitigation and Conservation Commission. He also served as chairman of the Southern Utah Wilderness Alliance.

In 2002, while on a working trip with Dan to the Middle East, Mr. Owens collapsed on a Tel Aviv beach and died of a heart attack. He is a man who literally gave his life in the pursuit of peace.

Mr. Owens is survived by his wife Marlene Wessel, and their children, Dr. Sara Ruth Owens, Elizbather Tew, H. Douglas Owens, Stephen W. Owens, and Edward Owens.

He is dearly missed by the Center for Middle East Peace staff, by lawmakers throughout Washington, leaders around the world, and the countless people whose lives he touched.

Major Events in Israeli and Palestinian History

November 29, 1947. UN General Assembly votes to partition the British-controlled area of Palestine into two states, one for the Jews, and one for the Arabs living there. Jews accept the plan, but the Arab world rejects it.

May 15, 1948. The British leave Palestine, and Israel declares statehood. Egypt, Syria, Jordan, Lebanon, Iraq, and Saudi Arabia declare war on Israel, and invade her.

April 3, 1949. Israel and Arab states agree to armistice. The Jewish state gains about 50 percent more land than had been allotted her by the UN Partition Plan, while Jordan, in violation of the Partition Plan takes control of the West Bank.

October 29, 1956. In retaliation for a series of escalating border raids from Egypt, as well as the closing of the Suez Canal to Israeli shipping, Israel, acting in cooperation with the French and British, invades the Sinai peninsula and occupies it for several months.

May 1964. The PLO, the Palestine Liberation Organization, is founded with the aim of destroying Israel. The 1968 Palestinian National Charter calls for Israel's liquidation.

May 1967. Egyptian President Gamal Abdel Nasser closes the Straits of Tiran to Israeli shipping and instructs the UN to immediately withdraw the peacekeeping force that was placed there after the Suez war.

June 5–11, 1967. The Six-Day War. Israel destroys the Egyptian and Syrian air forces on the war's first day, and occupies Sinai and Gaza. When Jordanian troops open fire on Israel, Israel goes in and conquers the West Bank, and then takes over the Golan Heights from Syria. UN Resolution 242 calls for Israel to withdraw from territories (not "the" territories) in return for peace with her Arab neighbors.

October 6, 1973. The Yom Kippur War. Egypt and Syria attack Israel on the Jewish Day of Atonement. Egypt takes control of the Suez Canal and Syria reconquers the Golan Heights. Following massive Soviet arms shipments to the Arab countries, and massive US resupplying to the Israelis, Israel succeeds in pushing back the Syrians and threatening Damascus. Ariel Sharon crosses the Suez Canal and cuts off the Egyptian Third Army.

March 26, 1979. A peace treaty is signed between Egypt and Israel.

June 7, 1981. Israel destroys Iraqi nuclear reactor.

October 6, 1981. Egyptian President Anwar Sadat is assassinated by radical Islamists while on the reviewing stand of a victory parade celebrating the Yom Kippur War.

June 6, 1982. Israel invades Lebanon in an effort to destroy the PLO.

September 13, 1993. Oslo Declaration of Principles. Israel and the PLO agree to mutual recognition.

September 28, 1995. Oslo Interim Agreement signed. The Palestinian Authority is established.

November 4, 1995. Israeli Prime Minister Yitzhak Rabin is assassinated by right-wing political extremist, Yigal Amir. Shimon Peres replaces Rabin.

June 1996. Likud leader Benjamin Netanyahu is elected Israeli prime minister, replacing Shimon Peres.

May 17, 1999. Israel elects Labor Party leader and former General Ehud Barak as prime minister. Barak promises to make rapid progress toward peace.

September 28, 2000. Ariel Sharon visits the Temple Mount and the visit is followed by large-scale Palestinian rioting, inaugurating the Second Intifada.

February 6, 2001. Ariel Sharon elected prime minister, replacing Ehud Barak. He promises "peace and security."

March–April, 2002. Saudi peace initiative adopted at Beirut Summit.

November 11, 2004. Palestinian Authority president Yasser Arafat dies.

January 9, 2005. Mahmoud Abbas (Abu Mazen) is elected president of the Palestinian National Authority.

Summer 2005. Israel evacuates Gaza (taking with her the 8,500 Jewish settlers resident there), and turns it over to the Palestinian Authority.

Speech by Prime Minister Ariel Sharon at the Caesarea Conference June 30, 2005

Since my first day in office, it was clear to me that we must not be satisfied with the status quo. I am not ready to sit and only put out fires and solve crises. That is not why I was elected.

I took the responsibility of initiating changes in every field where they were necessary, in order to lead Israeli society to a better situation for the future. We are in the midst of doing so....

The greatest change we are implementing is the Disengagement Plan. We had to take the initiative. We faced a situation in which we could be either leaders or be led. And we decided to lead. We decided what our priorities were—we are withdrawing from the Gaza Strip—an area where there was no chance of establishing a Jewish majority, and which would clearly, in any final agreement, not be part of the State of Israel. At the same time, we are directing the majority of our efforts to areas which are most crucial to ensuring our existence—the Galilee, the Negev, Greater Jerusalem, the settlement blocs, and the security zones.

I initiated the Disengagement, because it is the best tool to fundamentally change the national situation of the

State of Israel. Withdrawing from Gaza will have a positive and decisive influence on every facet of life in Israel: security, the economy, and the quality of life in the country. I say with confidence—the Disengagement places Israel in a better position in every possible scenario, and it will be carried out according to the timetable decided, beginning in seven weeks time.

The first challenge we face is the security challenge. Disengagement can assist us in curbing terror, and will certainly allow us to fight terror in a better and more effective way.

There is a real chance that Disengagement will encourage the Palestinian side to stop the terror offensive. For the first time the Palestinians will have to choose: Do they want to begin building, or continue destroying? Are they ready and able to change on their own, or do they want to continue to wallow in the swill of their hatred and incitement, which will lead their population to poverty and suffering? They truly have an opportunity. It would be regrettable if they miss it.

There exist in Palestinian society and its leadership moderate forces who want to make the right choice. Disengagement can help them, and constitutes a test of whether or not they can lead, whether we have or do not have a partner. If the Palestinians fail, and again choose the path of war and terror, the Disengagement will significantly improve our ability to deal efficiently with the terror.

The purpose of terror is, inter alia, to force the international community to actively intervene against Israel. Disengagement stopped this trend, and changed the political thought. Now it is clear to the world that Israel is ready to contribute its part by making genuinely painful concessions. Now, the nations of the world have directed their demands to the Palestinians—to dismantle the terror organizations, stop the incitement, introduce law and order, and focus on bolstering Palestinian society rather than destroying the State of Israel.

Disengagement fortified the strategic alliance between Israel and the United States. There is understanding between us and the Americans vis-a-vis the immediate, necessary steps, regarding advancing according to the outline of the Roadmap, and regarding an uncompromising demand that the Palestinians fulfill all their obligations in order to move forward.

However, more important than anything else is the understanding we reached with the Americans that, in negotiations for the final agreement, they will support our stand on two essential issues for ensuring our future—keeping the settlement blocs in Israeli territory and preventing the entry of Palestinian refugees into the State of Israel. And this, of course, in addition to a series of other topics which appear in the agreement between President Bush and me. No previous government was successful in obtaining such commitments from the American administration in the past.

These understandings, written commitments signed by the President of the United States, and later overwhelmingly endorsed by both Houses of Congress, are the best guarantee of ensuring the character of the State of Israel as a Jewish and democratic nation.

The Disengagement Plan is the basis for strategic change in the situation of the State of Israel, parallel with the changes taking place in the Middle East. We are already able to see a shift in our relations with Egypt, the most important of Arab nations. We saw a good example for that today, at the signing of the natural gas agreement.

Despite not being an essentially economic event, the Disengagement clearly has a large economic and social influence. I have heard claims that the money invested in the Disengagement Plan could have been invested in social issues. We should probably remind those who forgot that we, in the government and in the Knesset, decided to deviate from the budgeted deficit and government expenditure to fund the Disengagement because of its special character, and the fact that it is a one-time event. Therefore, I do not feel I need to explain here that investment in Disengagement could not be allocated to any other target. It is the realization of the Disengagement Plan which will allow for diverting resources which are currently earmarked for ongoing security, to be used in building Israeli society and narrowing the gaps in it. This is the right economic and social path.

I believe that Disengagement will be one of the most successful, economically influential steps carried out in Israel. It is sufficient to examine the influence which the Disengagement has had on the growth of the Israeli economy even before it is carried out. I believe that your experts estimated the benefits of Disengagement at 2 percent GNP per annum. There is no doubt that the dramatic increase in tourism, foreign investment, and consumption originate primarily in optimism in the political arena. It is no accident that in the past two years we have seen renewed growth and a return of foreign investors.

All this is even before we address your analysis of the nightmare of nonimplementation of the Disengagement Plan, with all the consequences that this will have on our political position and how we are treated in the global markets....

There are those, of course, who are directly hurt by change—any change. Such are the original residents of the Gaza Strip and northern Samaria, most of whom are wonderful people, the best of Israeli society. I feel their pain and respect their objections, even when they are extremely severe. I tell you that I love these people; I also love them when I hear the voices of pain and protest which are directed at me personally.

However, with all the pain and understanding, we must not be deterred from this crucial change. The fate of the entire state is at stake. We must withdraw from Gaza in order to build Israel.

I can tell you that a tremendous amount of work is being done to ensure that every resident who so wishes will find a solution which suits their needs, whether it be through financial compensation if that is what they wish, or by arranging temporary housing, or renting an apartment, or by preparing places for permanent settlement and land for agricultural cultivation.

There is a solution for all who wish it. There is a place for every evacuee—a place in Israel and a place in our hearts.

I make a complete distinction between them and the extremist gangs who are trying to terrorize Israeli society and tear it to pieces through violence against Jews and Arabs, and offending Muslims and violating their symbols, by thuggery and disobedience. It is not the path of Judaism. It is not the path of the settlers. It is not the path of Israel.

We will deal with these phenomena with a heavy hand since they threaten our very existence here, as a Jewish and democratic country. This is how we acted yesterday, and today at the hotel in Gush Katif which we evacuated. I wish to commend the Israel Police forces and IDF soldiers who carry out this difficult and important task. We will not let anyone raise a hand against an IDF soldier or a policeman in the Israel Police. Everyone who cares about this country—and who has public influence—must stand up and make a clear statement against these phenomena....

We face a difficult period of great internal pain. I am convinced that these are the labor pains of better times, in which we will stand, strong, united, and build a prosperous economy, a healthy, civilized, and more just society, and most importantly, in which we ensure the people of Israel a future of tranquility, security, and peace.

I am certain that, with God's help, we will succeed.

Thank you very much.

Index

ABOUT THE AUTHOR

S. Daniel Abraham, former chairman of Slim Fast, is the founder of the Center for Middle East Peace and Economic Cooperation in Washington, D.C., and a dedicated philanthropist devoted to Israel and Mideast peace. His other philanthropic projects address the needs of the homeless, terminally ill children, and abused children, as well as issues concerning education and nutrition. A New York native, he lives in Palm Beach, Florida.